USDA

United States Department of Agriculture

I0412172

Hazardous Fuels Management in Mixed Red Pine and Eastern White Pine Forest in the Northern Lake States: A Synthesis of Knowledge

Forest
Service

Northern
Research Station

General Technical
Report NRS-134

July 2014

Abstract

Fuels reduction decisions are made within a larger context of resource management characterized by multiple objectives including ecosystem restoration, wildlife management, commodity production (from timber to nontraditional forest products), and provision of recreation opportunities and amenity values. Implementation of fuels treatments is strongly influenced by their perceived influence on and compatibility with overarching management objectives. In some cases these objectives may be complementary while in others they may involve difficult tradeoffs. Such tradeoffs are only further complicated by institutional mandates, limited availability of information, and complex ownership patterns. Like natural resource managers across the United States, those in the northern Lake States must balance these competing demands as they seek to build their management programs. However, there is limited information available to support these management decisions in the mixed red (*Pinus resinosa* Ait.) and eastern white pine (*P. strobus* L.) forests of the northern Lake States.

This report informs fuels management decisions in the northern Lake States by synthesizing existing knowledge from the fields of silviculture, forest ecology, wildlife ecology, forest economics, public acceptance, and decision science. We provide an overview of forests and fire regimes in the northern Lake States followed by a description of different fuels treatment techniques and their expected outcomes. We then include a discussion of comprehensive management principles to consider in developing fire and fuels management programs for the region.

Authors

ERIC TOMAN is an associate professor at The Ohio State University, College of Food, Agricultural, and Environmental Sciences, School of Environment and Natural Resources, Columbus, OH.

DAVID M. HIX is an associate professor at The Ohio State University, College of Food, Agricultural, and Environmental Sciences, School of Environment and Natural Resources, Columbus, OH.

P. CHARLES GOEBEL is a professor at The Ohio State University, College of Food, Agricultural, and Environmental Sciences, School of Environment and Natural Resources, Wooster, OH.

STANLEY D. GEHRT is an associate professor at The Ohio State University, College of Food, Agricultural, and Environmental Sciences, School of Environment and Natural Resources, Columbus, OH.

ROBYN S. WILSON is an associate professor at The Ohio State University, College of Food, Agricultural, and Environmental Sciences, School of Environment and Natural Resources, Columbus, OH.

JENNIFER A. SHERRY is a Ph.D. candidate at Charles Sturt University, School of Environmental Sciences, Albury, New South Wales, Australia.

ALEXANDER SILVIS is a Ph.D. student at Virginia Tech University, College of Natural Resources and Environment, Blacksburg, VA.

PRISCILLA NYAMAI is a Ph.D. candidate at The Ohio State University, College of Food, Agricultural, and Environmental Sciences, School of Environment and Natural Resources, Wooster, OH.

ROGER A. WILLIAMS is an associate professor at The Ohio State University, College of Food, Agricultural, and Environmental Sciences, School of Environment and Natural Resources, Columbus, OH.

SARAH MCCAFFREY is a research forester with the U.S. Forest Service, Northern Research Station, Evanston, IL.

Cover Photo

Mixed-pine forest harvested using variable retention at Seney National Wildlife Refuge, Upper Michigan. Photo by Priscilla Nyamai, used with permission.

Manuscript received for publication January 2014

Published by:

USDA FOREST SERVICE
11 CAMPUS BLVD., SUITE 200
NEWTOWN SQUARE, PA 19073-3294

July 2014

For additional copies:

USDA Forest Service
Publications Distribution
359 Main Road
Delaware, OH 43015-8640
Fax: 740-368-0152

Visit our homepage at: **http://www.nrs.fs.fed.us/**

Hazardous Fuels Management in Mixed Red Pine and Eastern White Pine Forest in the Northern Lake States: A Synthesis of Knowledge

Eric Toman, David M. Hix, P. Charles Goebel, Stanley D. Gehrt, Robyn S. Wilson, Jennifer A. Sherry, Alexander Silvis, Priscilla Nyamai, Roger A. Williams, and Sarah McCaffrey

CONTENTS

OVERVIEW

Purpose of this Guide

Fire and fuels management is an inherently complex endeavor. The purpose of this guide is to provide a synthesis of the available literature to help inform the fuels management decisions of managers within the northern Lake States region. The forests of the northern Lake States occur within the Laurentian Mixed Forest Province (McNab et al. 2007) (Fig. 1). This region is dominated by a variety of ecosystem types that are characterized as fire-dependent including jack pine (*Pinus banksiana* Lamb.) forest ecosystem types; mixed-pine forest ecosystem types dominated by red pine (*Pinus resinosa* Ait.) and eastern white pine (*Pinus strobus* L.); mixed-pine and oak (*Quercus* spp. L.) forest ecosystem types; and peatland forest ecosystem types dominated by black spruce (*Picea mariana* (Mill.) Britton, Sterns & Poggenb.), tamarack (*Larix laricina* (Du Roi) K. Koch), and other woody plant species.

This report focuses on mixed red and eastern white pine dominated forests. This general classification includes the following forest types:
- Michigan Natural Features Inventory: dry northern forests and dry-mesic northern forests
- Minnesota DNR: northern dry-sand pine woodlands, northern poor dry-mesic mixed woodlands, northern dry-mesic mixed woodlands
- Wisconsin DNR: northern dry forest and northern dry-mesic forest

This report incorporates the knowledge and experience of scientists from a variety of backgrounds (silviculture, ecology, wildlife biology, behavioral science, and decisionmaking), resource managers, and fire practitioners who work in the northern Lake States. This is part of a larger effort, supported by the Joint Fire Science Program, to develop a more robust relationship between scientists and practitioners within the region to address current forest and fire management challenges. It is our goal that these efforts will support managers in their efforts to accomplish their objectives within the current complex decision-making environment.

This first section of this report provides an overview of ecological conditions in the Lake States region. The next section provides a summary of key principles to consider in developing fuels management programs. Drawing on a broad range of scientific research, we discuss integrating ecological principles into fire and fuels decisions, considerations in building public acceptance, and effects of treatments on wildlife habitat. The next section describes the different types of fuels treatments that can be used to reduce hazardous fuels. For each treatment, relevant scientific findings are presented on how the treatment: 1) reduces wildfire hazard, 2) affects wildlife habitat, 3) contributes to ecological restoration, and 4) is viewed by the public. We conclude with some summary comments and an appendix discussing research on the influence of fire on major wildlife taxonomic groups.

Figure 1.—Northern Lake States region.

Fire Management Context

Wildfire issues in the United States are generally perceived to be primarily important in western or southern states. However, recent fires have resulted in significant impacts within the study region. Between January 2002 and March 2011, Michigan, Minnesota, and Wisconsin experienced a combined 35,773 wildfires that burned 669,167 acres (NIFC 2011). Minnesota in particular has experienced substantial fire activity in recent years. In 2011, the Pagami Creek Fire burned more than 90,000 acres on the Superior National Forest resulting in the evacuation of both recreation users from the Boundary Waters Canoe Area and residents of nearby properties. In 2006, Minnesota also experienced the Cavity Lake Fire (31,830 acres) and the Ham Lake Fire that burned more than 75,000 acres and destroyed more than 130 structures. The Cottonville Fire in Wisconsin in 2005 burned 3,400 acres and destroyed 30 residences. In Michigan, recent large fires include the Meridian Boundary Fire, Hughes Lake Fire, Sleeper Lake and Stonington Fires.

Several federal agencies manage lands within the region; the U.S. Department of Agriculture Forest Service and the U.S. Department of Interior (DOI) Fish and Wildlife Service have the largest ownership while the DOI National Park Service, Bureau of Indian Affairs, and the Department of Defense manage smaller, but still significant, lands within the region. State agencies in Michigan, Wisconsin, and Minnesota also manage extensive areas dominated by fire-dependent forests. Tribal nations and nongovernmental organizations such as The Nature Conservancy (TNC) and other land trusts also manage fire-dependent forests within the study region. The remaining forests are in private ownership and managed according to the objectives of the property owner.

The complexity of these land ownership patterns complicates fire management. Public lands in the region are generally highly fragmented and Federal or State-owned parcels are intermixed with private property and rural neighborhoods. Thus, agency fuels-management activities are virtually assured of taking place in the public eye, creating challenges in understanding how the fire management problem is understood, what values are most at risk, and levels of citizen support for fuels treatments. In addition, such conditions mean that wildfires do not have to be very large or travel very far before directly impacting human developments. A recent review found that nearly all forests in the region are located within 25 km of densely populated communities (Radeloff et al. 2005). Moreover, in the Lake States region, humans are the primary cause of fires through both intentional and unintentional ignitions (Cardille and Ventura 2001).

Fire and fuels managers in the northern Lake States region must balance numerous competing demands as they seek to achieve multiple objectives including hazardous fuels reduction, ecosystem restoration, wildlife management, commodity production, and provision of recreational opportunities (Wilson et al. 2009). In some cases these objectives may be complementary (e.g., fuels treatments may provide improved habitat conditions) while in others they may involve difficult tradeoffs (e.g., the public may prefer thinning treatments over prescribed fire due to perceived risks to private property) (Toman et al. 2011).

Compared with other regions of the United States, fire and fuels management programs within the northern Lake States are in an early stage of development. For example, some National Forests within the region hired their first fuels planning personnel in the early 2000s. This is not to say the region lacks fire and fuels capacity as for several decades there have been individuals and organizations with substantial experience and knowledge regarding fire; however, the networks to share information between these individuals, to develop and test new information, and to plan and implement large-scale fuels management programs are less well developed than in other regions of the United States.

Background

Current ecological systems in the northern Lake States forests are the product of centuries of human and natural disturbances. Studies illustrate several differences between the pre-Euro-American landscape and current forest structure, diversity, complexity, and fire regime with cascading effects evident through the region's ecosystems, including on habitat patterns for wildlife, nutrient cycles, water flows, forest composition and structure, and terrestrial and aquatic species diversity (Drobyshev 2008a, Foley et al. 2005, Schulte et al. 2007). Early accounts by explorers and settlers, timber mill documentation, and original land surveys have been used to document the importance of mature and old growth forests in the eastern United States (Williams 1989). The pre-European settlement forest of the northern Lake States was dominated by red pine, but also included eastern white pine and jack pine (Whitney 1986) (Fig. 2). These fire-dependent ecosystems historically experienced frequent (once in 25-35 years) low-intensity fires, and less frequent large fires (once in 100 to 160 years) (Drobyshev 2008b, Frelich and Lorimer 1991, Gilmore and Palik 2006, Whitney 1986). Fire-adapted species such as red pine rely on both large and small fire events to control competing understory vegetation, expose mineral seedbeds, and open the canopy to promote seedling establishment (Ahlgren 1976, Gilmore and Palik 2006, Vogl 1970). Resident wildlife also relies on certain habitat conditions provided by fire-regulated forests. Fire promotes habitat diversity and maintains long-term stability in the system, thereby benefiting animals like the white-tailed deer and bobcat (Heinselman 1973).

In just over a century, human intervention greatly altered both forest structure and fire regimes in the northern Lake States. During the late 19th and 20th centuries, extensive and often wasteful logging was conducted throughout the region's deciduous forests (Williams 1989). Forest land was converted to agricultural land in many cases, although farming attempts were generally unsuccessful (Gough 1997) . In many pine lands, slash fires and catastrophic wildfires followed the harvesting and eventually lead to a push for fire suppression policies in the 1900s (Cleland et al. 2004, Schulte et al. 2007, Stearns 1997). When forests regenerated, a new forest structure emerged: red pine and eastern white pine stands decreased with the lack of natural fires, while the abundance and distribution of jack pine, fire-sensitive hardwoods, and other broadleaf deciduous species increased (Cleland et al. 2004, Drobyshev et al. 2008a,b). Where there once was variability in tree size and age distributions, the contemporary forests have become homogenized (Frelich 1995, Frelich and Lorimer 1991). The overall loss of compositional diversity, structural complexity, and age variability in northern Lake State forests has been accompanied by a shift in fire regimes (Frelich 1995,

Figure 2.—Old-growth mixed-pine forest ecosystem in the eastern Upper Peninsula of Michigan. Photo by Charles Goebel, used with permission.

Frelich and Lorimer 1991, Schulte et al. 2007). Average fire activity among all landscape ecosystem types has decreased dramatically, due at least in part to active fire suppression within the region (Drobyshev 2008a, Heinsleman 1973, Whitney 1986). However, as has been seen throughout the country, these changes have increased the potential for catastrophic fires in the future (Drobyshev et al. 2008a,b, Woodall et al. 2005). Current conditions within the region suggest there may be an increasing risk of major wildfires (Cardille and Ventura 2001, Haight et al. 2004). Many stands are vulnerable to wildfires as a result of insect outbreaks, major windstorms, or high stand densities (Hansen and Brand 2006, Miles et al. 2004, Perry 2006).

Fuels Treatments

Managers across the region are currently using a variety of fuels-treatment techniques to accomplish their objectives. Their primary techniques include thinning, mechanical, and fire treatments (including both prescribed fire and, in limited cases, wildland fire managed for resource objectives). Chemical treatments and livestock grazing have been used as well, but are not as common across agencies. Incorporating fire into forest management can be a practical method since fire was formerly a naturally occurring process that helped maintain open forest conditions and lower loads of hazardous forest fuels (Drobyshev et al. 2008b, Neumann and Dickmann 2001). Although naturally ignited wildfires and prescribed fires are generally recognized as useful tools, they often have a high risk associated with their implementation (Yoder 2008). Managers indicate they are limited in their ability to use fire by a lack of information about fire within the region's ecological systems, concerns about potential negative impacts to timber values, wildlife habitat, and private property (Corace et al. 2008, Palik and Zasada 2003, Wilson et al. 2009). In one of our included states, Michigan, an historical fire has also influenced the use of prescribed fire. In 1980, a USFS prescribed burn escaped and became the Mack Lake Fire that eventually burned 24,000 acres and 44 structures and resulted in one fatality. Although this fire occurred over three decades ago, it has had a long-term influence on manager decisions (Myer 2012) as well as citizen acceptance of the use of prescribed fires in lower Michigan (Winter et al. 2002).

Thinning and mechanical treatments may be used to emulate the effects of fires on ecosystems and reduce some of these risks and limitations (although they also have their own risks and limitations). Using two or more treatments together on the same stand may serve to reduce some of these associated risks and limitations. Ultimately, while there are several treatment options, developing effective fuels treatment plans will depend on a manager's ability to select the best treatment(s) for a specific stand, in the context of the landscape, under the given social conditions.

COMPREHENSIVE MANAGEMENT PRINCIPLES

Fire and fuels management are conducted within the broader context of natural resource management. While fuels-treatment decisions are often driven primarily by the objective of decreasing the likelihood of destructive wildfires, in many cases managers may also consider other objectives. In a study of managers within the region, Wilson et al. (2009) found that this range of objectives included restoration of ecosystem integrity, incorporation of public desires and building acceptance, and promotion of wildlife habitat. In this section, we describe connections between these three related objectives and the success of fuels management programs.

Integrating Ecological Knowledge into Fuels Treatment Programs

While the science of fuel treatments is not as advanced for the northern Lake States as in other regions of the United States, the available and growing information on current ecological conditions, existing deviations from the natural range of variability, as well as the likely outcomes of fuels treatments can provide a solid foundation to develop fuels treatment programs. Such an approach views fuels treatments within the larger context of ecological management and recognizes that these treatments can contribute to other goals. Moreover, fuels treatments have a greater likelihood of success when informed by the history of past practices that have contributed to ecological degradation and changes in current conditions. Indeed, Covington (2000) argues that developing fuels programs without this context is akin to "treating a symptom and not the disease." Ecological restoration provides a mechanism with which to treat the disease by focusing on restoring important ecosystem structures and functions that are often regulated by fire. To adequately restore an ecosystem, one must have an extensive understanding of the processes and interactions among components that shape the ecosystem. Fuel reduction treatments will offer greater ecological benefits when driven by ecological restoration principles and applied within a formal adaptive management context (Covington 2000). Moreover, fuel reduction treatments will be more effective when tailored to the ecological context for the particular stand that requires treatment rather than taking a "one-size-fits-all" approach (Agee and Skinner 2005, Brown et al. 2003). When viewed this way, fuel reduction treatments become a tool for an adaptive process that restores and enhances ecosystem structure and function.

Building Public Acceptance

Several recent federal initiatives (e.g., the National Fire Plan, Healthy Forests Restoration Act, and National Cohesive Wildland Fire Management Strategy) have focused on fire and fuels management. Two main themes run through these initiatives. First, they emphasize the use of fuel treatments to proactively manage vegetative conditions and reduce the risk of fire. Second, they recognize the wildland fire problem is extensive and solutions will require an unprecedented degree of collaboration with a broad array of stakeholders. In response, these policies encourage, and in some cases require, local partnerships to identify and accomplish fuel management objectives. Thus, resource professionals require an understanding of citizen awareness and acceptance of the fire risk and the tools available to help mitigate those risks. Given these conditions, fuel treatment programs require a supportive constituency to be successful.

A substantial body of research indicates that public acceptance of fuels treatments is generally strong across the United States (e.g., McCaffrey and Olsen 2012, Toman et al. 2013). While most research has been completed in the western United States, those studies completed in the Lake States suggests that while residents generally accept treatments, they appear more skeptical about the ability of managers to effectively implement treatments (e.g., Shindler et al. 2009, Vogt et al. 2005, Winter and Fried 2000, Winter et al. 2002). This appears to be particularly true for prescribed fire; in one study, 70 percent of participants from Michigan, Minnesota, and Wisconsin expressed moderate or great concern about the possibility of an escaped prescribed fire (Shindler et al. 2009).

Findings across this research suggest acceptance is influenced by: 1) awareness of the rationale behind fuel treatment activities; 2) trust in agencies and confidence in local managers to effectively implement treatments (as the treatments themselves carry their own risks and uncertainties); 3) the degree to which citizens have an opportunity to participate in fire planning; 4) citizen beliefs about the outcomes likely to result from treatments; and 5) public confidence that forest managers provide credible information regarding their fire and fuel management activities (e.g., Ascher 2010, Brunson and Shindler 2004, Loomis et al. 2001, Shindler and Toman 2003, Toman et al. 2011, Winter et al. 2002).

These findings emphasize the importance of working with local communities to build understanding of the fuels problem and expected outcomes of treatment use. Substantial research indicates that offering meaningful opportunities to participate in the planning process can increase understanding of treatment goals and objectives and build stronger trust between managers and local residents (see Shindler et al. 2002 for a review). In longitudinal research within the study region (comparing citizen responses in 2002 and 2008), trust in agency managers to effectively implement a treatment was the strongest predictor of its acceptance (Bennett 2010). However, over the study period, participants in the region expressed growing frustration with a lack of opportunities for citizen involvement in agency decision-making processes. While opportunities for citizen involvement do exist in each location as part of the agency planning process, responses here and elsewhere illustrate that citizens want an expanded role beyond what is typically available through standard scoping meetings. Successful efforts elsewhere have provided opportunities for face-to-face interactions between citizens and agency personnel including demonstration sites and field trips to treatment areas (Toman et al. 2006, Toman et al. 2008).

While engaging the public can seem like a daunting task, one possible approach is to engage local citizen groups such as watershed councils, friends and sportsman groups, and homeowner associations that are greatly concerned about forest conditions and usually have a stake in the outcomes. Working with these already established groups will provide access to local communication networks and can increase the effectiveness of agency outreach efforts.

Management of Wildlife Habitat

As managers develop strategies to reduce fire risk, they also must consider the potential effects different treatments may have on resident wildlife species. These species may be of interest because they are federally or state listed as threatened or endangered (e.g., Karner blue butterfly), they may be geographically restricted to the area (e.g., elk in some locations in the Lower Peninsula of Michigan), they may be game species with high recreation value (e.g., black bear), or they may be highly valued by the local community as nongame species (e.g., certain avian species such as Kirtland's warbler). It is important to recognize that fuels-management projects can also alter wildlife habitat. Fuels treatment decisions can be more effective when managers consider the outcomes of treatments for wildlife within the treated area.

While the literature review completed for this report is not definitive due to limited prior research in mixed pine forests of the northern Lake States region, we believe it provides an accurate representation of the current understanding of wildlife response to fuels treatments. By drawing on research from other regions, we identified expected response patterns. Some generalizations from this body of literature include:

- Direct mortality resulting from fuel reduction treatments on wildlife, such as burning from fire, trampling from equipment or people, or exposure to chemicals, is relatively minimal. The greater impact on wildlife is mostly indirect through the resulting habitat alteration. However, most information that comes from direct mortality is limited to anecdotal observations (Pilliod et al. 2006).

- Timing of fuel treatments will affect the extent of direct and indirect negative impacts on wildlife. For example, treatments implemented during the nesting season may inhibit reproduction and create a negative short-term response within species that might otherwise benefit from the treatment.

- Wildlife response to fuel treatments will usually reflect their natural history. Specifically, if a species is identified with early successional habitats, then they likely will respond positively (either numerically and/or functionally) to management that creates this habitat, regardless of the method that is used. Thus, over time fuel reduction treatments will likely produce habitat for wildlife that favor moderate to high disturbances, less complex structure, and a mosaic of disturbed and undisturbed forest to meet life history needs. Conversely, those species that favor large, dense patches of trees, heavy canopy cover, and more complex structure may lose habitat through fuel treatments.

- Some fuel treatments are likely to reduce snags, future snags, and downed wood that serve important forest ecosystem functions, and are important habitat features for many wildlife species. The retention of snags and some downed wood will likely reduce the negative effects of fuels treatment on wildlife species that depend on structurally diverse forests.

The expected outcomes of treatments on major wildlife groups are summarized below (additional information on taxonomic groups is available in the Appendix).

Large mammals: Fuels treatment will generally produce greater foraging habitat for large mammals in the mixed-pine forests of the Lake States, but mosaics of treated and untreated areas are most beneficial. Soft mast that is produced from enhanced herbaceous cover following fuels treatment is favored by black bears (Schwartz and Franzmann 1991), and the improved browse vegetation following treatment often benefits ungulates such as white-tailed deer (Jones et al. 2009,

Meek et al. 2008, Mixon et al. 2009). However, both species likely benefit from a mosaic of treated and untreated forest, with the untreated areas used for cover and alternate food. Bears will also use downed wood for foraging and winter dens. Deer are more likely to use treated areas if untreated areas are nearby.

Small to medium mammals: The small mammal community (e.g., shrews, rodents, hares and rabbits) in most forests is diverse; consequently, the short-term and long-term response to treatments is varied across species. Generalists usually experience a positive short-term response to treatment, and habitat specialists usually experience an initial negative response that shifts to positive over time. Species associated with closed canopies, such as northern flying squirrels, may be negatively affected by thinning (Meyer et al. 2007, Zwolak and Foresman 2007). As with larger mammals, small mammals and hares benefit from a patchwork of treated and untreated areas, and with the retention of coarse woody debris (Converse et al. 2006, Martell 1984, Zwolak and Foresman 2007). Little information is available for small-medium mammalian predators for any region.

Bats represent an important element of forest ecosystems. There is relatively little information on bat response to fuel treatments in the northern Lake States region, but general patterns emerge from other forest systems. They are likely to benefit from reduced structure at the secondary level, and a mosaic of treated and untreated areas (Loeb and Waldrop 2007). Fuel treatments may negatively impact bats through the loss of snags, as some bat species rely on these structures for summer roosting and reproduction. Conversely, prescribed fire may improve roosting habitat around remaining snags and create new potential roosts (Johnson et al. 2009, Lacki et al. 2009).

Avian species: Avian responses to fuel treatments have been highly variable among studies, often depending on the life history of species in question (e.g., ground or cavity nester) and the type, timing, and application of fuel treatments (see review in Saab and Powell 2005). General patterns that have been reported include: aerial, ground, and bark insectivores favor treated habitats; foliage gleaners favor untreated habitats; species with closed nests benefit from burn treatments more so than species with open-cup nests; and ground-nesters and canopy nesters favor burned habitat more so than shrub nesters. However, timing of the treatments is important, especially with regard to the nesting season. For example, ground nesters are negatively impacted by fuel treatments during the nesting season.

Cavity nesters (e.g., woodpeckers) can be negatively impacted by fuel treatments that remove snags and large-diameter trees. Treatments that can retain snags may benefit these species, although it is important to consider that simply maintaining a minimum number of snags may be insufficient because of the temporary nature of snags and the length of time required to replace them (Pilliod et al. 2006). Creation of snags by wildfires, when allowed to burn to meet fuel management objectives (i.e., fire use) can be especially important for some species, such as the black-backed woodpecker.

Raptor responses have not been studied, but it is likely that the responses of these species to fire are related to the availability of small mammalian prey. Fuel treatments may enhance foraging habitat for raptors by opening the understory, making prey more available. However, some raptors prefer closed canopies with a mixed understory. Additionally, fuel treatments that remove nesting structures may negatively impact some raptors.

Reptiles and Amphibians: There is relatively little information on the herpetofaunal response to fuel treatments in the northern Lakes States, or for more northern latitudes in general. Information from other regions indicates that reptiles likely benefit from warmer surface temperatures and enhanced prey availability resulting from fuel treatments, whereas most amphibians may have a negative or neutral response. Some studies have reported an immediate negative response to fire, likely due to direct mortality, but this was quickly reversed and a net positive response was observed thereafter. As with some small mammals, snakes and lizards benefit from retained coarse woody debris.

Amphibians that occur in upland forest habitats may experience direct mortality from fuel treatments and exhibit short-term negative responses. Many amphibians require cool, moist substrates or forest floors, and vegetative structure is beneficial for cover. Some toads may exhibit a positive response to prescribed burns and other treatments (Greenberg and Waldrop 2008, Kirkland et al. 1996).

CHARACTERISTICS OF WILDFIRE IN THE NORTHERN LAKE STATES

Fire and Fuels Issues in the Northern Lake States

Many natural and human activities have contributed to changes observed in the mixed-pine forests of the northern Lake States. Extensive turn-of-the-century logging followed by high severity stand-replacing fires significantly changed the ecological properties of the forest ecosystems (Cleland et al. 2004, Drobyshev et al. 2008a, Karamanski 1989). This era was followed by a prolonged period of fire suppression that modified the fire regimes from historical norms of frequent, low-severity surface fires. As a result, structural characteristics and species compositions of many forests have been altered well outside the historical natural range of variability (Schulte et al. 2007, Swain 1980, Whitney 1987). Lack of natural disturbances such as fire, which played an integral role in the regeneration of historically dominant species including red and eastern white

Figure 3.—Former mixed-pine forest now dominated by high fuel loadings of jack pine and fire-sensitive hardwoods. Photo by Charles Goebel, used with permission.

pine has resulted in a decline in the regeneration of these species (Ahlgren 1976, Cleland et al. 2004). Accompanying the decline in red and eastern white pine regeneration has been a gradual shift in species composition toward increasing abundance of shorter-lived pine species such as jack pine as well as fire-sensitive hardwood species such as red maple (*Acer rubrum* L.) (Friedman and Reich 2005, Sturtevant et al. 2009). An even greater consequence of the altered stand structures and species compositions has been increased accumulation of fuel loadings in these forest ecosystems. Currently, these forests consist of high densities of small trees, extensive ladder fuels and much greater fuel loads, on average, than the historical levels (Fig. 3) (Woodall et al. 2005). Due to these fuel levels, a critical concern to land managers is the potentially increased vulnerability of these ecosystems to intense stand-replacing crown fires (Cardille and Ventura 2001, Corace et al. 2009, Crow and Perera 2004).

To ensure clarity, we include definitions of several of the most commonly used terms (see sidebar) in discussions of fire characteristics and behavior in ecological systems (following Dickmann and Cleland [2002]).

Characteristics and Behavior of Fires in the Northern Lake States

Key terms (following Dickmann and Cleland [2002] and others as noted)

Crown fire-Fire that advances from top to top (or crown to crown) of trees or shrubs more or less independently of a surface fire.

Fire intensity-A general term referring to the heat energy released in a fire.

Fire return interval-Time in years between two successive fires in a designated area.

Fire occurrence (Fire frequency)-Number of fires per unit time in a specified area; the reciprocal of mean fire interval. (In this report, fire occurrence and fire frequency are used to refer generally to the temporal aspect of fire regimes.)

Fire regimes: Fire regimes refer to all those characteristics of fire, including fire intensity, frequency, season, size, and extent, that result in particular fire effects in a given biogeographical region (Graham et al. 2004). A number of approaches have been used to characterize historical fire regimes. Dendrochonology, which involves dating fire scars, is one technique that is commonly used (Drobyshev et al. 2008b, McEwan et al. 2007). The characteristics of fire regimes obtained from using these techniques are usually accurate and are often consistent with the understanding of stand development patterns in the areas of study. However, several factors affect fire regimes, including frequency and seasonality of ignition, flammability of living and dead plant material, vegetative structure including fuel ladders and tree spacing, landscape patterns and spatial heterogeneity, and weather conditions (Sousa 1984). Another important component of the fire regime is the frequency with which fire returns to an ecosystem; this temporal measure is influenced by ecological conditions and anthropogenic interventions within the specific area (Dickmann and Cleland 2002).

Fire rotation (Fire cycle)-Length of time necessary for an area equal to the entire area of interest (i.e., the study area) to burn (syn. fire cycle). Size of the area of interest must be clearly specified. This definition does not imply that the entire area will burn during a cycle; some sites may burn several times and others not at all. Fire cycles are usually determined by calculating the average stand age of a forest whose age distribution fits a negative exponential or a Weibull function (Van Wagner 1978).

Fire severity- Degree of impact of a fire on soils, vegetation and other ecosystem components (USFS 2003)

Fuel- Combustible forest materials (USFS 2003)

Ground fire-Fire that burns the organic matter in the soil or organic horizons that supports glowing combustion without flame; e.g., litter and duff, punky wood, tree roots, peat, or muck. This term often is mistakenly used to refer to a surface fire, although some surface fires can become ground fires.

Mean fire interval-Arithmetic average of all fire intervals determined, in years, in a designated area during a specified time period; size of the area and the time period must be specified.

Stand-replacing fire-Fire that kills all or most living overstory trees in a forest and initiates establishment of regeneration. This type of fire can be a ground, surface, or crown fire, but it is usually a combination of two or more types.

Surface fire-Fire that burns only surface fuels such as litter, other loose debris on the soil surface, and small vegetation. All wildland fires except those that smolder in snags or punky trees struck by lightning begin as surface fires.

Before Euro-American settlement, fire regimes of the mixed-pine forest ecosystems in the region were complex and heterogeneous, depending on local interactions between climate, physiography, soils, vegetation, and human factors (Cleland et al. 2004, Heinselman 1973). Many mixed-pine forest ecosystems in the northern Lake States experienced relatively frequent low-severity and non-stand-replacing surface fires that burned at intervals of 3 to 40 years (Dickmann and Cleland 2002, Drobyshev et al. 2008b), while others experienced more severe stand-replacing fires. In a fire-history (1707-2006) study of red pine-dominated forests at the Seney National Wildlife Refuge in the Upper Peninsula of Michigan, Drobyshev and colleagues (2008b) found that while large fires (>1100 ha) had occurred in this area, small fires (<100 ha) dominated the fire regime. These fires, which originated from lightning and recurrent ignitions by indigenous people, left the basic structure of the overstory unaltered or created small gaps and maintained a relatively open understory. However, many fire-history studies have found relatively high variability in fire return intervals across different historical time periods, land-use patterns, and landform types. With the emphasis on complete fire suppression, there has been a general decrease in fire frequency in this region.

Occurrence: Despite some regional constraints on the occurrence of wildfires, certain "hotspots" in the general area of the northern Lake States experienced frequent burning prior to Euro-American settlement, as well as large wildfires following settlement (Cleland et al. 2004, Scheller et al. 2008). These hotspots are mostly associated with the drier glacial landforms, such as sandy outwash plains, where coniferous and other flammable vegetation are found (Cleland et al. 2004, Drobyshev et al. 2008a). Cardille and Ventura (2001) provide very useful information on the occurrence of contemporary wildfire in a Lake States fire database that puts together extensive fire information from one Federal and three State agencies. Several other studies have also documented changes in fire regimes in this region pre- and post-European settlement (Cleland et al. 2004, Drobyshev et al. 2008a,b). For example, while Drobyshev et al. (2008b) found seasonal fire distributions to be moderately prevalent around the late season, in a study on fire occurrence between the period of 1985 and 1995, Cardille and Ventura (2001) found that the average annual number of fires was 1,683, with more than 70 percent of these occurring in the months of April and May. They also found that forests dominated by eastern white pine, red pine, and jack pine were more likely than other forest types to have had at least one fire during the study period as well as larger fires compared with the other forest types.

Causes: Prior to Euro-American settlement, fires in northern Lake States mixed-pine ecosystems originated from both natural (lightning) and anthropogenic (Native Americans) sources (Loope and Anderton 1998). Fires from both origins played a large role in forest dynamics during this period, driving succession and hindering the development of fire-intolerant species (Loope and Anderton 1998, Whitney 1986). With Euro-American settlement, there was extensive timber harvesting often followed by intense slash fires and clearing for agriculture. Some studies have investigated the role of environmental and social factors in influencing current wildfire occurrence in forest ecosystems in Minnesota, Wisconsin, and Michigan (Cardille et al. 2001, Cardille and Ventura 2001). Results indicate that more than 80 percent of fires between 1985 and 1995 were of human origin. More than a third of the fires were from debris burning (burning of material from land clearing, dumps, and trash), while nearly 30 percent were intentionally ignited. These studies suggest that fire potential within this region is influenced by both natural conditions and human settlement and resulting activities. The high levels of flammable fuels in forest systems, accumulation of litter on the forest floor, and the vertical structure of fuels leading to "fuel ladders," contribute to concerns about the potential for intense fires in these ecosystems (Cleland et al. 2004).

Fuel loadings: The presence and spatial distribution of fuels in any given forest ecosystem affect fire behavior (Graham et al. 2004). Characteristics of fuels, including composition, moisture content, amount, and structure affect how fires will burn and the resulting impact on the environment (Agee 2002, Albini and Reinhardt 1995). Common categories of fuels include:

> *Ground fuels:* Roots of trees, woody material integrated into the soil surface, and organic soil horizons (duff) make up what is referred to as ground fuels (Sandberg et al. 2001). Deep layers of continuous ground fuels are common in forests that have not experienced fire for a long time (Graham et al. 2004). Given that the organic material in the soil layers usually does not burn intensely, ground fires can smolder for many days or weeks, particularly

if the initial moisture contents are high (Frandsen 1991, Hungerford et al. 1991). As such, ground fires are very likely to damage soils and roots of trees (Marshall et al. 2008, Ryan and Noste 1983, Ryan and Reinhardt 1988).

Surface fuels: Surface fuels are composed of litter, grasses, shrubs, and all woody material that is lying on, or in contact with the ground (Sandberg et al. 2001). Along with weather conditions, surface fuel characteristics such as surface fuel bulk density, size-class distribution, depth, and continuity influence the intensity and the spread of fire in a given forest ecosystem type (Graham et al. 2004). Surface fires typically consume vegetation in the understory while the overstory tree crowns usually do not burn, except for under unusually dry and windy conditions (Marshall et al. 2008) or when surface fuel loadings are substantially high, for example due to slash left on the site following harvesting and thinning operations.

Ladder and crown fuels: Crown fuels refer to all fuel materials that are suspended above the ground on trees and other vegetation (Graham et al. 2004). In addition to live and dead tree branches, the shrubs and small tree layers form "ladder fuels" which create continuity from the surface fuels to canopy fuels, allowing fires to reach canopies and become crown fires. Crown fires are intense and move fast, often resulting in large burned areas (USFS 2003). Continuity and density of the canopy trees, and wind conditions contribute to the rate at which fire moves and spreads in the canopy.

FUELS TREATMENT TECHNIQUES AND EFFECTS

In this section, we describe the most commonly used techniques (prescribed fire, wildfire use, thinning, combined treatments) for fuels management in mixed pine forests of the northern Lake States and discuss their potential effects on key objectives (reduction of wildfire hazard, provision of wildlife habitat, ecological restoration, and incorporate public desires) for each method.

Prescribed Burning

Prescribed burning can be an effective technique to achieve several management objectives in mixed-pine stands, including reducing fuel loadings. In the region, the type of prescribed burning most frequently used in the region is surface fire. Backing fires are often recommended to consume organic matter accumulations (fuel loads) and limit the risk of future severe fires.

Prescribed burning may prevent the establishment of certain woody plant species and can be used to selectively kill the aboveground portions of certain species and individuals in the smaller size classes (Rouse 1988). The severity of a surface fire determines the resulting damage to ecosystem components; therefore, low- to moderate-intensity burning is recommended. Although prescribed fire can damage trees, mature red pine are resistant to fire injury because of their thick bark (Hauser 2008, Starker 1934), apparently more so than eastern white pine (Starker 1934, Van Wagner 1970).

Prescribed burning may scorch the bark and lower branches of some trees. In Ontario, Canada, Van Wagner (1972) found that as the intensity of prescribed burning increased, the scorch heights also increased in a mature red and eastern white pine stand. Using headfires, if the flame lengths did not exceed 4 feet in height, the crowns were left untouched; however, where the flames were up to 8 feet, all the foliage was scorched as high as 50 feet above ground. In both cases, the wind speed was light and the duff moisture content was less than 40 percent. Methven (1971) reported a similar relationship but with less scorching due to the larger diameter trees in their study. In a 47-year-old red pine plantation in Minnesota that experienced a wildfire, Sucoff and Allison (1968) found that mortality was closely related to percentage of needles killed; 40 percent of trees with more than 95 percent needles killed experienced mortality.

There are several silvicultural uses of prescribed burning in mixed-pine forests. Perhaps the most important is a reduction in hazardous fuels. Burning breaks up the "fuel ladder" consisting of needles and leaves draped in the lower branches of shrubs and trees, though in mixed-pine stands this type of situation is not common (Van Wagner 1970). Periodic, moderate intensity fire may be used to control understory development when managing for red pine and eastern white pine (McRae et al. 1994).

Under specific conditions of weather and fuel moisture, summer burns in mature stands are prescribed in the years prior to harvesting to eliminate shrubs and reduce duff layers (Ek et al. 2006). Prescribed fires can also be used as site preparation treatments to help regenerate conifers by preparing the seedbed (Alexander et al. 1979, Duchesne and Hawkes 2000). Along with the use of machines to scarify the seedbed, mineral soil is exposed in patches, which is necessary for the germination of light-seeded species such as red pine (Zasada et al. 2004). This practice of soil scarification provides the correct conditions for natural regeneration of red pine (Ek at al. 2006). To prepare the seedbed, remove aboveground portions of competing vegetation. McRae et al. (1994) suggests that flame lengths should not exceed 3 feet to prevent crown scorching mature red pines.

Dickmann (1993) reviewed the fire ecology of red pine forests and discussed potential opportunities to use fire treatments to achieve management objectives. Dickmann concludes that low intensity burns are unlikely to negatively impact overstory tree growth, soil structure, nutrients, water quality, or water movement. However, higher intensity fires may result in increased crown scorch and nutrient loss. Additional research indicates that while young red pine stands are susceptible to fire injury, prescribed fire can be used effectively in the larger poletimber- and sawtimber-sized stands to control understory development and reduce the risk of wildfires (Benzie and McCumber 1983).

Reduction of wildfire hazard: In their seminal paper, Agee and Skinner (2005) presented the basic principles of forest fuels reduction treatments. When restoring the resilience of fire-dependent forests, they stressed that prescribed fire is effective at reducing surface fuels by consuming some of the biomass. The potential flame length is shorter, and fire in these stands will be easier to control (Agee and Skinner 2005). On the other hand, depending upon fire intensity, more fuels will be created as understory shrubs and small trees are killed (Brown 2009). It is also possible that a surface fire of moderate intensity will scorch the lower branches of trees resulting in an increase in the height to the base of live tree crowns, as the hot gases rise above the flames (Van Wagner 1970).

In a mixed-pine stand the thickness of the organic matter accumulation can be reduced using prescribed burning (Gilmore and Palik 2006). In pole- and sawtimber-size stands, the trees are less susceptible to fire injury (Benzie and

McCumber 1983) and periodic prescribed burning can control build-up of fine fuels and help reduce the risk of wildfire (Benzie 1977). Summer burns can consume the forest floor and expose mineral soil in patches (Alban 1977). As the weather conditions and the moisture contents vary, the fire will likewise produce different results. In an Ontario, Canada study, Van Wagner (1963) found that only when the duff moisture content was less than 40 percent and the fire danger rating was at least "high" was the entire duff layer removed and mineral soil exposed. In another study in the Ottawa River Valley of Canada, Van Wagner (1972) used prescribed fire on a red and eastern white pine stand growing on sandy loam till soil. With more intense prescribed fire, the mineral soil was exposed on up to half of the study area. In eastern Upper Michigan, Drobyshev et al. (2008a) found duff depth and fine fuel loadings were lower in stands with a history of periodic burning.

Prescribed burning does have the effect of reducing the shrub vegetation layer in mature mixed-pine stands (Gilmore & Palik 2006, Rudolf 1990, Van Wagner 1970). Summer burns in Minnesota proved more effective than spring burns in both killing the aboveground parts of shrubs (e.g., beaked hazel [*Corylus cornuta* Marsh.] and reducing resprouting (Alban 1977). Buckman (1964) concluded that a single summer or fall burn of at least moderate intensity when the humus was dry would eliminate beaked hazel, as was possible using multiple burns. In Ontario, the beaked hazel in the understory of an 80 year-old mixed-pine stand was practically eliminated on two sites after two consecutive annual burns (Van Wagner 1963). In general, Duchesne and Hawkes (2000) stated that two successive burns might be required to eradicate understory competition, particularly beaked hazel, and expose bare mineral soil. Gilmore and Palik (2006) recommend summer burns conducted over several growing seasons to control dense shrub competition and expose mineral soil.

Provision of wildlife habitat: Limited research has been done on the effects of prescribed fire on wildlife in mixed-pine forests. Accordingly, it was frequently necessary to draw from the published literature on southwestern and southeastern conifer forests to gain insight into possible treatment effects on wildlife in the mixed-pine forest ecosystems. For the purposes of this guide, we use the traditional meaning of wildlife to include terrestrial and avian vertebrate species, excluding fish and invertebrates. A description of the methods used to complete the literature review and a description of fire effects on specific taxonomic groups is presented in the Appendix.

Prescribed fire generally occurs at lower temperatures than wildfires and subsequently creates a less diverse habitat mosaic. However, increases in herbaceous growth following prescribed fire can benefit a number of game species, specifically white-tailed deer (*Odocoileus virginianus*) and elk

(*Cervus canadensis*) (Jones et al. 2009, Meek et al. 2008, Mixon et al. 2009). Generally, prescribed fire intensity is low enough that changes in habitat occur only in the short-term, such that most species of mammals experience no significant lasting effects from prescribed fire (Kalcounis et al. 2008, Matthews et al. 2009, Simon et al. 2002). Game species such as white-tailed deer, elk, moose (*Alces alces*), black bear (*Ursus americanus*) and turkey (*Meleagris gallopavo*) exhibit positive responses to prescribed fire in the short term, and little evidence suggests any negative long term effects (Jones et al. 2009, Main and Richardson 2002, Mixon et al. 2009, Schwartz and Franzmann 1991, Van Dyke and Darragh 2007).

Ecological restoration: There is broad agreement that some form of restoration is needed for many forest ecosystems (Brown et al. 2004), and that many of the structural components of a fire-resilient forest provide the basis of forest ecosystem restoration plans (Agee and Skinner 2005). One principle of managing for a fire-resilient forest as highlighted by Agee and Skinner (2005) is to maintain large trees as they are typically the most fire-resistant. Large trees also have the highest bases to their crowns, thus reducing ladder fuels. A key point in utilizing some form of prescribed fire as a fuels treatment is that it represents a reintroduction of a natural process that is a critical component in driving ecosystem dynamics, especially in low-severity and mixed-severity fire-dependent forest ecosystem types (Brown et al. 2004, DellaSala et al. 2003).

While prescribed burning has been applied widely as a restoration practice across fire-dependent forests of the western United States, its application in mixed-pine forest ecosystems of the northern Lake States has been limited. Despite this lack of direct information from the region, we can surmise some potential advantages and disadvantages of using prescribed burning to treat fuels within a restoration framework. In terms of advantages, the application of prescribed burning improves a variety of ecosystem conditions that favor the establishment of important species, especially red pine and eastern white pine. When applied in this fashion, several prescribed burns may be necessary depending on the amount of understory competition. The initial burn is often utilized to reduce fuels and it is usually recommended that this initial burn be conducted when fuels are still green in the early spring to reduce crown scorch and bole damage. Sometimes a second summer burn, conducted shortly after the initial burn, can be an effective restoration method, especially during years with good cone and seed production. However, there must be surface fuels on site to help carry these summer burns. Prescribed burning conducted in the spring can also reduce the susceptibility of red pine to red pine cone beetles as they overwinter on the forest floor (Miller 1978). Prescribed burning may also be more economical than other treatment methods, even for small stands (McRae 1979), and may enhance understory species richness and diversity (Webster 2008).

There are also potential issues with the application of prescribed burning within an ecological restoration context. When applied too broadly as a restoration treatment, prescribed burning has the potential to homogenize the landscape and can damage important wildlife habitat (Tiedemann et al. 2000). Prescribed burning implemented to reduce fuel loadings can also kill large trees that are intended to be retained as seed trees or to provide structure in the treated or restored stand (Agee 2003). Consequently, the use of prescribed burning as a fuel reduction treatment within an ecological restoration context is often most successful when linked with thinning treatments that reduce ladder fuels (Brown et al. 2004).

Incorporate public desires: Substantial research across the United States demonstrates that citizens with higher fire-related knowledge are more supportive of fuels management activities such as prescribed fire and thinning programs (see summaries in McCaffrey and Olsen 2012, Toman et al. 2013). Moreover, public understanding and acceptance of fuel treatments has steadily increased over time. Early studies found that citizens generally overestimated the negative impacts of fire; not surprisingly, a majority preferred complete fire suppression (Stankey 1976). However, as awareness has increased regarding the role of fire in the landscape, acceptance of management use of fire has also grown (Toman et al. 2013). Several studies over the past decade have found acceptance for some use of both prescribed fire and thinning to reduce fuel loads near 80 percent (e.g., Absher and Vaske 2006, Lim et al. 2009, McCaffrey 2006, McCaffrey et al. 2008, Toman et al. 2011, Vogt et al. 2007). While much of this research has been completed in other regions of the United States, a recent study suggests similar results in the Lake States (Shindler et al. 2009).

Despite the growing acceptance of prescribed fires, the public still has some reservations with its use. Residents have indicated concerns with the potential for an escaped prescribed burn, increased prevalence of smoke, increased erosion, reduced water quality, and negative impacts on wildlife habitat (Blanchard and Ryan 2007, McCaffrey 2006, Shindler and Toman 2003, Winter et al. 2002). These concerns appear particularly strong in the northern Lake States where 70 percent of participants indicated a moderate or great concern with prescribed fires getting out of control (Shindler et al. 2009). Other concerns were also prevalent as more than 40 percent expressed concerns for increased soil erosion, loss of fish and wildlife habitat, damage to private property, increased levels of smoke, reduced scenic quality, and economic loss of useable timber. Concerns were significantly greater among residents of Michigan with some results suggesting this may be associated with the lasting influence of the Mack Lake Fire (an escaped prescribed fire in Michigan's northern Lower Peninsula) (Winter et al. 2002).

While such concerns may seem to argue against the use of prescribed fire, it is also important to note that the public also recognizes potential beneficial outcomes from prescribed fires. Findings from Michigan found at least half of the study participants agreed that prescribed fires were very likely to improve forest conditions, restore forests to more natural conditions, result in less smoke over time, and save money (Winter et al. 2006). These results paint a somewhat nuanced picture regarding the use of fire within the region with residents recognizing that prescribed fires could result in positive outcomes while also indicating the treatments themselves carry some risk of negative impacts. Having said that, even with such concerns a strong majority of residents living near forested areas within the region have expressed support for some use of prescribed fire; 38 percent agreed it was a legitimate tool that should be used anywhere, while another 44 percent indicated it should be used in carefully selected areas (Shindler et al. 2009). These results suggest a cautious support for prescribed fire use within the region that can provide a foundation for success. In the final section of this document, we discuss key points to consider for efforts to build continued acceptance of fuels programs.

Wildland Fire Managed for Resource Objectives

In certain situations, naturally ignited fires may be managed to accomplish resource objectives. The term for this practice can differ based on agency and region, but for the purposes of this guide we refer to it as "wildland fire," or "wildland fire managed for resource objectives." This treatment is most likely to be used in remote areas where potential of damage to private property is low. Given the patterns of property ownership within the Lake States region, there are limited locations where this treatment is likely to be used.

Reduction of wildfire hazard: The current use of wildland fire in mixed-pine stands to reduce fuels seems to be very limited or nonexistent and its effects have not been documented within the region. In other areas, the use of wildland fire results in variable fire behavior and mixed effects (Hunter et al. 2007).

Provision of wildlife habitat: Limited research has examined the effects of wildland fires managed to achieve resource benefits within the study region. In this section we draw on a larger body of literature examining the effects of wildfire on wildlife. Response of wildlife to wildfire tends to be more varied than response to prescribed fire. This is largely due to the variable effects of wildfire on wildlife habitat. Specifically, wildfire tends to burn more intensely and creates more substantial, longer-lasting habitat changes than prescribed fire. This is neither inherently good nor bad from a wildlife community standpoint. Rather, it is best thought of as a community modifier, creating dynamic long-term shifts in species composition as habitat structure changes following high intensity alteration. See Appendix for a description of fire effects on specific taxonomic groups.

Of the large taxonomic groups reviewed, birds had the widest range in responses to wildfire. Generally, we conclude that wildfire will change avian community composition in both the short and long term. However, community composition in wildfire areas should revert to prefire composition as habitat returns to prefire conditions (Haney et al. 2008, Hobson and Schieck 1999). Changes in community composition are largely driven by cavity-nesting and bark-foraging species, such as the black-backed woodpecker (Apfelbaum and Haney 1981, Hutto 1995, Nappi and Drapeau 2009). Increases in these species tend to be relatively short-lived, with spikes in abundance in the first 3 years following wildfire and decreasing thereafter (Murphy and Lehnhausen 1998, Nappi and Drapeau 2009). Beyond cavity-nesting and bark-foraging species, reductions in habitat closure tend to benefit open-foraging species (Bock et al. 1978, Bock and Bock 1983). Ground-nesting species may be expected to decline immediately following wildfire as suitable cover decreases.

Mammalian responses to wildfire are also varied, but generally appear to be neutral or positive in the short term. However, it is important to note that there are few long-term studies on mammal species following wildfire, and thus the ultimate outcome is unknown for most species (Fisher and Wilkinson 2005). If avian communities are an indicator, mammalian communities likely revert to prefire composition in the long term.

As previously noted, virtually no research has been conducted on herpetofauna in the mixed-pine forests, leaving the responses of reptiles and amphibians to wildfire virtually unknown. However, if responses to prescribed fire are extrapolated, we predict that reptiles will benefit from increased thermal opportunities while amphibians will suffer from loss of cover and moisture retaining refugia (Greenberg and Waldrop 2008, Jones et al. 2000).

Ecological restoration: As mentioned previously, the fire regimes of the mixed-pine forest ecosystems in the northern Lake States are complex and heterogeneous, depending on local interactions between climate, physiography, soils, vegetation, and human factors (Cleland et al. 2004, Heinselman 1973). According to Hanies et al. (1975) and Lorimer and Gough (1988), the fire season spans from April to October, with peak incidence before leaf-out in the spring or in the autumn. While a restoration-based approach to fuels treatment should attempt to emulate the heterogeneity associated with the natural fire regime, this may not be a realistic practice in the current landscape. Due to effective fire control that began in the early 20th century and continues today, the number and size of fires have declined dramatically (Keane et al. 2008). Consequently, an increase in fire occurrence that could serve as the foundation of a wildland fire approach is not expected due to an increase in the abundance of shade-tolerant species in the understory and shifts towards a less fire-prone state (Frelich and Reich 1995, Nowacki and Abrams 2008). Furthermore, the fragmentation of the current landscape will make it difficult to implement adequate wildland fire policies to effectively restore ecosystem conditions, including reducing fuel levels.

Incorporate public desires: Limited research has examined public perceptions of the application of wildland fire to achieve resource objectives. Those studies completed to date were all conducted outside the Lake States region. One study of National Forest visitors in California, Colorado, and Washington found most did not support this practice even when with minimal projected impacts (including low risk of private property damage, no impact on air quality) and a quick forest recovery (Kneeshaw et al. 2004). It is likely that this treatment will raise similar, but potentially stronger, concerns as the use of prescribed fire. In particular, citizens are likely to be concerned about the potential for these fires to burn out of control leading to damage to both private property and natural systems. Having said that, as with prescribed fire use, these concerns do not necessarily mean citizens will not support this practice. Rather, they point to the importance of building awareness of the rationale behind such treatments, expected outcomes, and developing strong relationships with local residents. Indeed, recent findings from two case studies in California and Wyoming found that community members expressed a range of preferences for management of recent fires from full suppression to fire use (Steelman and McCaffrey 2011). Moreover, in the one location where agencies had worked before the fire to explain why wildland fire use was an appropriate approach participating members of the public understood the value of this approach and were more accepting of its use. These findings suggest that citizen understanding and acceptance of the use of wildland fire to achieve resource benefits may be malleable over time.

Thinning

Thinning is a silvicultural tool that can be used to optimize tree or stand growth, reduce crown fuels, and manage for biodiversity, wildlife habitat, and aesthetics (Gilmore et al. 2005). Thinning is an intermediate treatment aimed primarily at controlling the diameter growth of trees by reducing the stand density. While thinning techniques have been traditionally used to increase the commercial value of managed stands, they can also be used to achieve fuels reduction objectives. By modifying the stand density and arrangement of remaining trees, thinning treatments can influence fire spread, behavior, and intensity. There are many methods of thinning, with most approaches based on the crown class positions of the trees and (or) the spatial pattern of the remaining trees. The three most common types of thinnings in mixed pine forests (Buckman et al. 2006) are as follows:

1. Low thinning (or thinning from below), in which trees are removed from the lower crown classes, resulting in acceleration of the natural mortality of these individuals.

2. Crown thinning (or thinning from above) is a much different approach. Trees of the upper crown classes are harvested to favor the development of the most promising codominant and dominant trees. This approach provides the potential for increased economic return as the removed trees are typically larger and potentially more valuable than those removed in low thinning. It also results in a stratified residual stand with an upper stratum of the favored dominants and codominants above a lower stratum of overtopped trees.

3. Mechanical thinning is more common in plantations or dense stands. In many cases, the thinning approach may be based on some geometric pattern or spacing of the residual trees. Sometimes these simple thinning approaches are known as 'mechanical' thinning, given that they are applied in routine, straightforward ways. Two commonly used types of mechanical thinning include 'strip' and 'row' thinning. Strip thinning is typically used in extremely dense, young stands using a machine (e.g., bulldozer) to destroy trees in narrow lanes. While a drastic approach, strip thinning reduces stagnation in the stand and permits other later thinnings by creating access lanes within the stand. Row thinning is often conducted in plantations of pine species. Depending on the desired level of removal and the age of the plantation, a set pattern will be established and whole rows of planted trees will be harvested (e.g., every second or third row).

As a main component of the planned silvicultural system for a given forest stand, there is often a predetermined sequence and schedule of thinning methods. A recently developed handbook for red pine stands provides a general guide for management actions based on the condition of the stand or management objectives (Gilmore and Palik 2006). Buckman et al. (2006) recently summarized many of the growth and yield studies for red pine in the Lake States. To keep future options open, they state that most managers will plant at initial densities of 600 to 1,200 trees per acre (approximately 6- to 8-ft spacing), and reduce the density following thinning to 110 to 140 ft^2/acre. Crown thinning of red pine stands at low- or medium-levels of stand density results in greater growth compared to low thinning methods (Buckman et al. 2006); however, at higher residual stand densities (greater than 120 ft^2/acre) there were no apparent differences in several long-term research studies.

Reduction of wildfire hazard: Removing trees with low bases of live crowns (or low, dead branches), typical of overtopped crown class trees, will reduce ladder fuels and wildfire hazard. If unmerchantable small trees are also removed manually or with equipment, the effect will be to increase the canopy base height which can reduce the potential for crown fires and canopy damage due to scorch (Agee and Skinner 2005). In the low thinning method, the removal of trees in the lower crown classes decreases the stand density and increases the spacing between trees resulting in reduced likelihood of a crown fire. The larger, relatively more fire-resistant trees will remain following thinning. In contrast, during crown thinning the emphasis is placed on releasing the crowns of dominant and codominant trees, and the smaller overtopped and intolerant crown class trees are not harvested. While such approaches may reduce canopy density, the focus on trees in the upper canopy will not influence the risk of a crown fire in the lower canopy. Row and strip approaches break up the continuity of fuels; however, smaller trees with the potential to serve as ladder fuels will remain in untreated areas within the residual stand after thinning. While research examining the effectiveness of thinning approaches to reduce fire risks in red and white pine forests is limited, it is likely that low thinning will provide greater reduction of risk that the other approaches as has been found in other forest types (Agee and Skinner 2005).

Variable-retention harvesting has also been evaluated in the Lake States as a method for regenerating multi-cohort, mixed-species red pine forests (Palik and Zasada 2003). In variable-retention harvests, the overstory trees are left either with uniform spacing (dispersed retention) or in an aggregated pattern. It has been hypothesized that the pattern of overstory retention will have a significant effect on the distribution of fuels (Gilmore and Palik 2006, Palik and Zasada 2003).

In addition to influences on the forest canopy, resiliency to fire may also be influenced by the particular techniques used to remove the biomass from the treated stand. Conventional harvesting approaches often emphasize removal of the main tree stem while the tree tops and branches are left behind on the forest floor. Given enough time, this material would eventually decay and contribute to increased fuels on the forest floor particularly as it dries (Agee and Skinner 2005, Duvall and Grigal 1999). In addition, this slash can create a travel hazard for both recreational uses and equipment movement and provide an obstacle to planting or to natural regeneration. Managers may want to prioritize slash removal from some treated areas based on management objectives (e.g., where regeneration is a priority) or along roads and trails where impacts to travel and risks of fire starts, including arson, may be greatest.

Methods to address slash include modifying its structure and composition on-site or removing it from the stand. Lopping and scattering the slash by hand or mechanical means is one approach to modify the fuels left on-site by severing branches and tops of a certain minimum size to better consolidate the material on the forest floor (within 2 to 4 feet) and distributed it throughout the stand. Fire may also be used to treat slash remaining on site following a thinning or other mechanical treatment. Broadcast burning, where fire is intentionally started and burns woody debris as it lies on the ground throughout a stand, may be used in clearcut areas. This approach may also be used in thinned stands when fuel loads are low enough, the stand structure is appropriate (e.g., adequate spacing between remaining trees, absence of ladder fuels), and the remaining forest species are fire resistant. Managers may also spot burn piles of slash made by machines or by hand following harvesting activity. In most cases, pile burns require less personnel and equipment than broadcast burns. As for the timing for such burns, conifer slash may be burned very soon after harvesting, while the slash of hardwood species needs several weeks to cure (Ek et al. 2006).

Slash may also be removed from the stand following treatment. In some cases, the slash may be disposed of at a landing where it may be chipped for removal in trailer trucks for utilization elsewhere. For example, if markets allow, the resulting chips may be used for bioenergy production. In cases where utilization is economically unfeasible, the chips may be burned on-site after the logging is completed in order to clear the landings. While reducing fuels within a stand, removing the logging slash in addition to the main stems of harvested trees (e.g., whole tree harvesting) could also result in negative impacts. The small logs resulting from thinning may serve increase the amount of coarse woody debris, providing valuable wildlife habitat and return nutrients to forest floors in mixed-pine stands (Duvall and Grigal 1999). Work elsewhere suggests whole tree harvesting may negatively impact the long-term productivity of forest stands as nutrients are removed from the system (Walmsley et al. 2009).

Provision of wildlife habitat: Thinning of red pine in Michigan resulted in strong positive responses in ungulates (deer, elk), likely due to increased forage resources and hiding cover (Bender et al. 1997). Other research has identified mixed results in response of small mammal species to thinning treatments (Bender et al 1997, Converse et al. 2006). Wildlife responses to thinning may decline 4 to 5 years post-thinning as the canopy closes; thus, periodic thinning may be necessary if continued wildlife use is a management priority (Bender et al. 1997).

An advantage of thinning over burning may be the ability to selectively retain snags or coarse woody debris that benefit certain wildlife species (Ucitel et al. 2003). For example, black bears appear to benefit from habitat shifts to early successional stages that provide forage and cover during the active season, but that benefit can be maximized by also retaining hollow logs which are used for denning during winter (Pilliod et al. 2006). Likewise, targeted retention of snags will benefit some bats and cavity-nesting birds.

Ecological restoration: The use of thinning as a tool for fuels reduction within an ecological restoration framework is an acceptable practice that can help restore stand structure (Agee and Skinner 2005). As many mixed-pine forest ecosystems of the region developed in response to mixed-severity fires, thinning practices such as low thinning (or thinning from below) can emulate the outcomes of low- to moderate-severity fires (Gilmore and Palik 2006). When viewed in this manner, thinning can help develop a fire-resilient stand typical of those of the pre-Euro-American landscape through reducing live fuels in the understory and subcanopy, and enhancing stand structure to be more similar to that of old-growth or reference ecosystems. In particular, to increase ecological diversity, thinning projects can be planned to 1) emulate gap dynamic processes and strive for a variety in gap size and shape in a manner similar to the heterogeneous nature of stand structure following low- to moderate-severity fires, and 2) stress the retention of biological legacies to maintain and enrich stand structural complexity (Gilmore and Palik 2006).

Currently there is little information on specific approaches to thinning mixed-pine forest ecosystems to help reduce fuel loadings in the northern Lake States and the consequences of these activities. Recent investigations that utilize variable-retention harvests to reduce fuels but also develop multi-cohort, mixed-species forests may provide guidance on how thinning should most effectively be applied (e.g., uniform or in an aggregate pattern) to restore forest structures and processes that will help reduce fuel loadings naturally (Gilmore and Palik 2006, Palik and Zasada 2003).

Incorporate public desires: Similar to prescribed fire, public acceptance of thinning has been studied in multiple locations across the United States. These studies have found high levels of acceptance of thinning in most locations. Compared with prescribed fire, most locations had a higher proportion of residents offer full rather than more qualified acceptance for the use of thinning (see reviews in McCaffrey and Olsen 2012, Toman et al. 2013). Also, as noted previously, some studies have found thinning treatments were preferred over prescribed fire near WUI communities (Bright and Newman 2006, Brunson and Shindler 2004, Ryan et al. 2006). Specific to the study region, Shindler et al. (2009) also found strong support for the use of thinning to reduce fuels in the Lake States. Fifty-nine percent gave agency managers full discretion to use thinning to reduce fuels wherever they see fit while another 28 percent indicated thinning should be used in carefully selected areas. Another study found that 55 percent of Michigan participants approved of the use of mechanical treatments (Winter et al. 2006). Regarding potential outcomes of thinning treatments, two-thirds of Michigan residents indicated thinning would very likely provide for the extraction of wood products while just over half indicated such treatments would save money by reducing the cost of fighting future wildfires (53 percent) and have a negative impact on scenery (53 percent) (Winter et al. 2006). Fewer felt these treatments were very likely to improve wildlife conditions (44 percent) or restore forests to a more natural condition (37 percent).

Other Mechanical and Combination Techniques

Besides tree removal, other mechanical approaches or combined mechanical and fire approaches may be used to reduce fuels (particularly surface or ladder fuels). Heavy equipment may be used to reduce fuel loads, alter fuel composition, and allow access for replanting a treated stand (Guries 2002). Machines may be used to uproot and chop apart small trees and understory vegetation; the resulting material may then be crushed and incorporated into the soil. Roller chopping involves using large drums filled with water and fitted with blades that are pulled by a bulldozer may also be used to break up slash. Specialized bulldozer blades (e.g., root rakes or KG blades) may be also used to break off and uproot remaining vegetation. Dragging anchor chains with a bulldozer across the stand is a mechanical treatment that has been used for the purposes of scarifying the soil and breaking up the continuity of fuels (Brown 2009). Harvesting machinery or tractors may be fitted with specialized blades to masticate slash and, in some cases, understory vegetation including shrubs and small trees. The treated material remains on-site in pieces of varying sizes depending on the type of equipment used. The use of these mechanized site preparation techniques may be expensive, and care must be taken to minimize negative effects on the upper soil horizons and forest floor. In addition, some understory shrubs and trees may resprout after being treated through mechanical means and treatments will likely need to be repeated at 2- or 3-year intervals in red pine stands (Ek et al. 2006).

Reduction of wildfire hazard: Limited research has examined the effectiveness of these alternative approaches on fuel hazard reduction in the Lake States. Removal of slash will reduce the fuels available to carry a fire. Other treatments, such as lopping and scattering or roller chopping will break the remaining slash into smaller pieces and increase decomposition rates. If a fire does occur, these alternative treatments may also alter the resulting fire behavior by removing ladder fuels and, thus, leading to a surface fire instead of a crown fire.

However, in some cases, these alternative treatments may actually contribute to increased fuel loads. A key finding from a study of eastern white pine stands in northeastern Wisconsin found that surface fuels increased after broad-spectrum herbicide application in August followed one month later by a mechanical treatment consisting of dragging anchor chains (by a bulldozer) (Brown 2009). In this case, a moderate to high density of hardwood saplings were killed by the treatment and became 10- and 100-hr fuels. Such findings emphasize the importance of tailoring the selected fuels reduction approach to the specific conditions of the stand being treated.

Provision of wildlife habitat: As with the previous sections, limited research has examined the effects of alternative mechanical treatments on wildlife in mixed-pine forests. Thus, it was necessary to draw from the published literature from other regions. Short-term effects of mechanical removal to wildlife would involve species that may be directly impacted by trampling and disturbance of coarse woody debris (which serve as refuge and source of food). In general, these are considered minimal for all vertebrate groups when compared to indirect effects of changes in habitat structure and composition (Pilliod et al. 2006).

One study of combined fuel treatments in deciduous Appalachian forests describes responses of small mammals. Treatments included prescribed burning, mechanical felling of shrubs and small trees, and a combination of burning and mechanical felling treatments. Comparisons of wildlife abundance between treatments yielded no short-term (1 to 2 years) differences in abundance or use patterns for the white-footed mouse (*Peromyscus leucopus*), a generalist species, despite differences in surface structure (Greenberg et al. 2006). There was also little short-term difference in herpetofaunal response to mechanical or combined burn-mechanical treatments, although there was a trend toward increasing abundance (Greenberg and Waldrop 2008).

Ecological restoration: From an ecological restoration perspective, the most effective restoration plans are those that focus on practices that emulate natural disturbances. Thinning followed by prescribed fire has been effectively used as a fuels reduction and restoration treatment in fire-dependent forest ecosystems of the western United States (Brown et al. 2004), as well as the northern Lake States. Often for the restoration of red pine, prescribed fire is used in concert with the shelterwood or seed-tree regeneration method, and one or two prescribed fires may be needed depending on the amount of understory competition.

Other combined techniques have been less successful as restoration treatments. For example, in mesic white pine stands in Wisconsin, Webster (2008) found that stands treated mechanically and with herbicides were less diverse and had higher densities of woody seedlings than stands treated with prescribed fire only, with red maple composing over 75 percent of this regeneration. Additional research on combining mechanical and other techniques is needed in order to understand the role these practices may have on reducing fuels and restoring important ecosystem processes.

Incorporate public desires: In general, public acceptance for a combined approach is likely to be based on acceptance of the specific treatments employed. Many of the alternative mechanical methods discussed here are not likely to be familiar to the public. While limited data is available, citizens are likely to have concerns with impacts from the use of heavy equipment to treat forested stands. Research has found high levels of support for a combined thinning and prescribed fire approach in Minnesota (Vining and Merrick 2008) as well as beyond the Lake States region (Blanchard and Ryan 2007, Kent et al. 2003).

Other Fuels Treatment Technique —
Chemical Treatment and Livestock Grazing

Herbicides may be used to control unwanted (or undesirable) vegetation, e.g., ferns, herbs, grasses, sedges, and woody plants (trees, shrubs, and vines). Human safety is the foremost concern in all use of these chemicals, which must be correctly applied by properly trained personnel following the directions on the label. The applicator may need to be certified or licensed in some states. The formulation of herbicide, i.e., its solubility in water or in oil, will depend upon the target plant species and the method of application to be used. A number of chemicals are labeled for use in mixed-pine stands in the Lake States. Broadcast methods are used to cover large treatment areas quickly and effectively. The spraying may be either from the air or ground-based. Soil application of a water-soluble herbicide that is taken up by the root systems may also be used. In some cases, plants may be treated individually with herbicide through stem injection, basal spraying, or stump surface treatments. The effectiveness of herbicides can be increased when used following cutting of unwanted vegetation to prevent resprouting.

Domestic animals such as cattle or goats may also be used to reduce certain types of fuels in mixed-pine stands. For instance, Benzie and McCumber (1983) reported that trials in Minnesota used cattle to control the growth of vegetation, as well as prepare planting sites. Grazing can lead to mixed results as the grazing animals will selectively target preferred vegetation. Moreover, it is important to not graze during spring bud break, as new, green shoots of conifers may be edible and browsed by domestic animals. Grazing can also result in some trampling damage and soil compaction.

Reduction of wildfire hazard: Herbicides may be used to control competing vegetation, which will indirectly reduce fuel loadings. Where feasible, although relatively high in cost, their use will result in greater selectivity among species and much less resprouting.

The use of domestic animals as a fuels treatment technique seems to be a viable approach in theory; however, to it has received limited attention within the region. Research from other regions found grazing animals could have mixed effects, increasing fine fuels and potential for fire frequency in some cases (Borman 2005), while decreasing fine fuels and defoliating flammable shrubs and deciduous trees in others (Bachelet et al. 2000). The specific results were influenced by the ecological system and available vegetation, the grazing species, and the intensity of grazing (see summary in Hunter et al. 2007). These results emphasize the importance of conducting additional trials within the region if grazing is considered for fuels reduction efforts.

Provision of wildlife habitat: Little information is available on comparative effects of chemical fuel treatments relative to other types or controls for wildlife. Possible direct negative effects for wildlife through exposure to chemicals are generally considered to be temporary (Guynn et al. 2004). Alteration to stand structure and composition from chemical treatments are more long term and generate mixed responses from wildlife species (Guynn et al. 2004), similar to mechanical treatments. Evidence from other pine ecosystems suggests that forest floor small mammals exhibited no difference in abundance between traditionally thinned and chemically treated treatments while medium and large herbivores (lagomorphs and ungulates) exhibited both positive and negative responses to chemical treatments and suggested chemical treatments could be managed to benefit each of these species groups if an aggregated pattern of crop trees was maintained following treatment (Sullivan et al. 2002).

Ecological restoration: While the use of herbicides is a commonly accepted practice in ecological restoration, they are most commonly used to control nonnative and invasive species. When compared with other practices that are available to help control competition (i.e., prescribed burning), the use of herbicides represents a more active intervention with limited reliance on natural processes. In most cases, unless direct human intervention is necessary to reintroduce and maintain natural processes, managers prefer a more passive restoration approach to remove activities causing restoration and allow natural processes to return. However, in some cases, current forest structure will need to be modified before natural processes can again be effective at restoring conditions. The use of herbicides, grazing, or other alternative practices may provide a means to modify these systems to a condition where a more natural fire regime is possible.

Incorporate public desires: Limited research examines the acceptance of grazing or herbicide treatments; the few studies that have been completed were conducted outside of the region. Existing studies on grazing suggest it is a generally acceptable practice with large majorities accepting at least some amount of grazing to reduce fuel levels (Brunson 2008, Brunson and Shindler 2004, McCaffrey 2008). Acceptance is much lower for herbicide use and large proportions of respondents consider it unacceptable (Bowker et al. 2008, Brunson 2008, McCaffrey 2008, Monroe et al. 2006, Toman et al. 2011). A telephone survey found that only 24 percent of the general public in the northeastern United States agree that land managers should use chemical treatment to control ground vegetation as part of a wildfire management program (Bowker et al. 2008).

CONCLUSIONS

Today's hazardous fuels reduction programs are completed within the broader context of resource management. While a primary goal is to manage stand conditions and reduce the likelihood of a catastrophic wildfire, managers must also balance other objectives including promotion of wildlife habitat and diversity, restoration and protection of ecosystem integrity, protection of public safety, provision of forest products, protection of private property, and consideration of public desires. Developed by a team of scientists with expertise in these topic areas and in cooperation with managers from across the region, this report provides a summary and synthesis of the currently available literature to inform fuels management decisions within mixed-pine forest ecosystems of the northern Lake States.

Fire and fuels management personnel within the region have had substantial success developing fuels management programs to date and this report is one component of ongoing efforts to support further success in the future. Many of these efforts are coordinated through the Lake States Fire Science Consortium – a network of fire managers and scientists in the fire dependent ecosystems in the Lake States Region. Please see the Consortium website for additional information about products and activities within the region (http://lakestatesfiresci.net/).

LITERATURE CITED

Absher, J.D.; Vaske, J.J. 2006. **An analysis of homeowner and agency wildland fire mitigation strategies.** In: Peden, J.G.; Schuster, R.M., eds. Proceedings of the 2005 Northeastern Recreation Research Symposium. Gen. Tech. Rep. NE-341. Newtown Square, PA: U.S. Department of Agriculture, Forest Service, Northeastern Research Station: 231-236.

Agee, J.K. 2002. **The fallacy of passive management: Managing for firesafe forest reserves.** Conservation Biology in Practice. 3:18-25.

Agee, J.K. 2003. **Monitoring postfire tree mortality in mixed-conifer forests of Crater Lake, Oregon.** Natural Areas Journal. 23:114-120.

Agee, J.K.; Skinner, C.N. 2005. **Basic principles of forest fuel reduction treatments.** Forest Ecology and Management. 211: 83-96.

Ahlgren, C.E. 1976. **Regeneration of red pine and white pine following wildfire and logging in northeastern Minnesota.** Journal of Forestry. 74:135-140.

Alban, D.H. 1977. **Influence on soil properties of prescribed burning under mature red pine.** Res. Pap. NC-139. St. Paul, MN: U.S. Department of Agriculture, Forest Service. 8 p.

Albini, F.A.; Reinhardt E.D. 1995. **Modeling the ignition and burning rate of large woody natural fuels.** International Journal of Wildland Fire. 5(2):81-92.

Alexander, M.E.; Mason, J.A.; Stocks, B.J. 1979. **Two and a half centuries of recorded forest fire history.** Sault Ste. Marie, Ontario: Environment Canada, Forestry Service, Great Lakes Forest Research Centre. 2 p.

Apfelbaum, S.; Haney A. 1981. **Bird populations before and after wildfire in a Great Lakes pine forest.** The Condor. 83:347-354.

Artman, V.L.; Downhower, J.F. 2003. **Wood thrush *(Hylocichla mustelina)* nesting ecology in relation to prescribed burning of mixed-oak forest in Ohio.** The Auk. 120:874-882.

Arvai, J.; Gregory, R.; Ohlson, D.; Blackwell, B.; Gray, R. 2006. **Letdowns, wake-up calls, and constructed preferences: People's responses to fuel and wildfire Risks.** Journal of Forestry. 104(9):173-181.

Ascher, T. 2010. **Factors influencing support for prescribed burning and mechanical thinning among wildland-urban interface residents in the lake Tahoe basin.** Columbus, OH: Ohio State University. M.S. thesis.

Bachelet, D.; Lenihan, J.M.; Daly, C.; Neilson, R.P. 2000. **Interactions between fire, grazing and climate change at Wind Cave National Park, SD.** Ecological Modeling. 134:229-244.

Ballard, W.B.; Krausman, P.R.; Boe, S.; Cunningham, S.; Whitlaw, H.A. 2000. **Short-term response of Gray Wolves, *Canis lupus*, to wildfire in northwestern Alaska.** Canadian Field-Naturalist. 114:241-247.

Bender, L.C.; Minnis D.L.; Haufler, J.B. 1997. **Wildlife responses to thinning red pine.** Northern Journal of Applied Forestry. 14:141-146.

Bennett, J. 2010. **Longitudinal analysis of public response to wildland fire and fuel management: Examining citizen responses and fire management decisions from 2002 – 2008.** Columbus, OH: Ohio State University. 149 p. M.S. thesis.

Benzie, J.W. 1977. **Manager's handbook for red pine in the north-central states.** Gen. Tech. Rep. NC-33. St. Paul, MN: U.S. Department of Agriculture, Forest Service, North Central Research Station. 22 p.

Benzie, J.W.; McCumber, J.E. 1983. **Red pine.** In: Burns, R.M., eds. Silvicultural systems for the major forest types of the United States. Agric. Hndbk. 445. Washington DC: U.S. Department of Agriculture, Forest Service: 89-91.

Blake, J.G. 1982. **Influence of fire and logging on nonbreeding bird communities of ponderosa pine forests.** The Journal of Wildlife Management. 46:404-415.

Blanchard, B.; Ryan, R.L. 2007. **Managing the wildland-urban interface in the northeast: Perceptions of fire risk and hazard reduction strategies.** Northern Journal of Applied Forestry. 24(3):203-208.

Bock, C.E.; Bock J.H. 1983. **Responses of birds and deer mice to prescribed burning in ponderosa pine.** The Journal of Wildlife Management. 47:836-840.

Bock, C.E.; Raphael M.; Bock J.H. 1978. **Changing avian community structure during early post-fire succession in the Sierra Nevada.** The Wilson Bulletin. 90:119-123.

Borman, M.R. 2005. **Forest stand dynamics and livestock grazing in historical context.** Conservation Biology. 19:1659-1662.

Bowker, J.M.; Lim, S.H.; Cordell, H.K.; Green, G.T.; Rideout-Hanzak, S.; Johnson, C.Y. 2008. **Wildland fire, risk, and recovery: Results of a national survey with regional and racial perspectives.** Journal of Forestry. 106:268-276.

Bright, A.D.; Newman, P. 2006. **How forest context influences the acceptability of prescribed burning and mechanical thinning.** In: McCaffrey, S.M., ed. The public and wildland fire management: Social science findings for managers. Gen. Tech. Rep. NRS-1. Newton Square, PA: U.S. Department of Agriculture, Forest Service, Northern Research Station: 47-52.

Brown, J.K.; Reinhardt, E.D.; Kramer, K.A. 2003. **Coarse woody debris: managing benefits and fire hazard in the recovering forest.** Gen. Tech. Rep. RMRS-105. Fort Collins, CO: U.S. Department of Agriculture, Forest Service, Rocky Mountain Research Station. 16 p.

Brown, M. 2009. **Low-intensity fire in eastern white pine: A supporting role in understory diversity.** Joint Fire Science Program, Fire Science Brief. 52: 6. Available at http://www.firescience.gov/projects/briefs/00-2-35_FSBrief52.pdf (Accessed August 25, 2011).

Brown, R.T.; Agee, J.K.; Franklin, J.F. 2004. **Forest restoration and fire: principles in the context of place.** Conservation Biology. 18:903-912.

Brunson, M. 2008. **Gauging the acceptability of fuels management: A matter of trust.** Western Rural Development Center Rural Connections. 1(3): 2-4.

Brunson, M.W.; Shindler, B.A. 2004. **Geographic variation in social acceptability of wildland fuels management in the western United States.** Society & Natural Resources. 17(8):661-678.

Buckman, R.E. 1964. **Effects of prescribed burning on hazel in Minnesota.** Ecology. 45:626-629.

Buckman, R.E.; Bishaw, B.; Hanson, T.J.; Benford, F.A. 2006. **Growth and yield of red pine in the Lake States.** Gen. Tech. Rep. NC-271. St. Paul, MN: U.S. Department of Agriculture, Forest Service, North Central Research Station. 114 p.

Cardille, J.A.; Ventura, S. J. 2001. **Occurrence of wildfire in the northern Great Lakes Region: effects of land cover and land ownership assessed at multiple scales.** International Journal of Wildland Fire. 10:145-154.

Cardille, J.A.; Ventura, S. J.; Turner, M.G. 2001. **Environmental and social factors influencing wildfires in the upper Midwest, United States.** Ecological Applications. 11(1):111-127.

Cleland, D.T.; Crow, T.R.; Saunders, S.C.; Dickmann, D.I.; Maclean, A.L.; Jordan, J.K.; Watson, R.L.; Sloan, A.M.; Brosofske, K.D. 2004. **Characterizing historical and modern fire regimes in Michigan (USA): A landscape ecosystem approach.** Landscape Ecology. 19:311-325.

Cleland, D. 2009. **The Great Lakes landscape: understanding historic and modern fire. Joint Fire Science Program,** Fire Science Brief. 33:2-5.

Converse, S.J.; White, G.C.; Farris, K.L.; Zack, S. 2006. **Small mammals and forest fuel reduction: national-scale responses to fire and fire surrogates.** Ecological Applications. 16:1717-1729.

Corace, R.G.; Goebel, P.C.; Seefelt, N.E. 2008. **Innovative forest management: Seney National Wildlife Refuge and Kirtland's Warbler Wildlife Management Area.** Forest Wisdom. 9:4, 10.

Covert-Bratland, K.A.; Block, W.M.; Theimer, T.C. 2006. **Hairy woodpecker winter ecology in ponderosa pine forests representing different ages since wildfire.** The Journal of Wildlife Management. 70:1379-1392.

Covington, W.W. 2000. **Helping western forests heal.** Nature. 408:135-136.

Crow, T.R.; Perera, A.H. 2004. **Emulating natural landscape disturbance in forest management-an introduction.** Landscape Ecology. 19:231-233.

Cunningham, S.C.; Ballard, W. 2004. **Effects of wildfire on black bear demographics in central Arizona.** Wildlife Society Bulletin. 32:928-937.

Cunningham, S.C.; Ballard, W.B.; Monroe, L.M.; Rabe, M.J.; Bristow, K.D. 2003. **Black bear habitat use in burned and unburned areas, central Arizona.** Wildlife Society Bulletin. 31:786-792.

Cunningham, S.C.; Kirkendall, L.; Ballard, W. 2006. **Gray fox and coyote abundance and diet responses after a wildfire in central Arizona.** Western North American Naturalist. 66:169-180.

Dees, C.S.; Clark, J.D.; Van Manen, F.T. 2001. **Florida panther habitat use in response to prescribed fire.** Journal of Wildlife Management. 65:141-147.

DellaSala, D.A.; Martin, R.; Spival, T.; Schulke, B.; Bird, M.; Criley, C.; VanDaalen, J.; Krelick, R., Brown; Aplet, G. 2003. **A citizen's call for ecological forest restoration: forest restoration principles and criteria.** Ecological Restoration. 21:14-23.

Dickmann, D.I. 1993. **Management of red pine for multiple benefits using prescribed fire.** Northern Journal of Applied Forestry. 10:53-62.

Dickmann, D.I.; Cleland D.T. 2002. **Fire return intervals and fire cycles for historic fire regimes in the Great Lakes region: a synthesis of the literature.** Unpublished manuscript.

Drobyshev, I.; Goebel P.C.; Hix, D.M.; Corace, R.G.; Semko-Duncan, M.E. 2008a. **Interactions among forest composition, structure, fuel loadings and fire history: A case study of red pine-dominated forests of Seney National Wildlife Refuge, Upper Michigan.** Forest Ecology and Management. 256:1723-1733.

Drobyshev, I.; Goebel P.C.; Hix, D.M.; Corace, R.G.; Semko-Duncan, M.E. 2008b. **Pre- and post-European settlement fire history of red pine dominated forest ecosystems of Seney National Wildlife Refuge, Upper Michigan.** Canadian Journal of Forest Research. 38:2497-2514.

Duchesne, L.C.; Hawkes, B.C. 2000. **Fire in northern ecosystems.** In: Brown, J.K.; Smith; Kapler, J, eds. Wildland fire in ecosystems: effects of fire on flora. Gen. Tech. Rep. RMRS-GTR-42-vol. 2. Ogden, UT: U.S. Department of Agriculture, Forest Service, Rocky Mountain Research Station. 35-51.

Durbian, F.E. 2006. **Effects of mowing and summer-burning on the Massasauga *(Sistrurus catenatus).*** American Midland Naturalist. 155:329-334.

Duvall, M.D.; Grigal, D.F. 1999. **Effects of timber harvesting on coarse woody debris in red pine forests across the Great Lakes states, U.S.A.** Canadian Journal of Forest Research. 29:1926-1934.

Ek, A.R.; Katovich, S.A.; Kilgore, M.A.; Palik, B.J. 2006. **Red pine management guide.** U.S. Dept. of Agriculture, Forest Service, Northern Research Station. Available at http://www.nrs.fs.fed.us/fmg/nfmg/rp/docs/rp_all.pdf (Accessed Sep. 9, 2011).

Ellison, L.N. 1975. **Density of Alaskan spruce grouse before and after fire.** The Journal of Wildlife Management. 468-471.

Fischer, R.A.; Wakkinen, W.L.; Reese, K.P.; Connelly, J.W. 1997. **Effects of prescribed fire on movements of female sage grouse from breeding to summer ranges.** The Wilson Bulletin. 109:82-91.

Fisher, J.T.; Wilkinson, L. 2005. **The response of mammals to forest fire and timber harvest in the North American boreal forest.** Mammal Review. 35:51-81.

Foley, J.A.; DeFries, R.; Asner, G.P.; Barford, C.; Bonan, G.; Carpenter, S.R.;
    Chapin, F.S.; Coe, M.T.; Daily, G.C.; Gibbs, H.K.; Helkowski, J.H.;
    Holloway, T.; Howard, E.H.; Kucharik, C.J.; Monfreda, C.; Patz, J.A.;
    Prentice, I.C.; Ramankutty, N.; Snyder, P.K. 2005. **Global consequences of
    land use.** Science. 309:570-574.

Fox, J.F. 1978. **Forest fires and the snowshoe hare-Canada lynx cycle.**
    Oecologia. 31: 349-374.

Frandsen, W.H. 1991. **Burning rate of smoldering peat.** Northwest Science.
    65:166-172

Frelich, L.E. 1995. **Old forest in the Lake States today and before European
    settlement.** Natural Areas. 15:157-167.

Frelich, L.E.; Lorimer, C.G. 1991. **Natural disturbance regimes in hemlock-
    hardwood forests of the Upper Great Lakes region.** Ecological
    Monographs. 61:145-164.

Frelich, L.E.; Reich, P. 1995. **Neighborhood effects, disturbance, and
    succession in forests of the western Great Lakes region.** Ecoscience.
    2: 148-158.

Friedman, S.K.; Reich, P.B. 2005. **Regional legacies of logging: departure
    from presettlement forest conditions in northern Minnesota.** Ecological
    Applications. 15: 726-744.

Geluso, K.N.; Bragg, T.B. 1986. **Fire-avoidance behavior of meadow voles
    (Microtus pennsylvanicus).** American Midland Naturalist. 116: 202-205.

Gilmore, D.W.; O'Brien, T.C.; Hoganson, H.M. 2005. **Thinning red pine
    plantations and the Langsaeter hypothesis: A northern Minnesota case
    study.** Northern Journal of Applied Forestry. 22: 19-26.

Gilmore, D.W.; Palik, B.J. 2006. **A revised managers handbook for red pine
    in the North Central Region.** General Technical Report NC-264. St. Paul,
    MN: U.S. Department of Agriculture, Forest Service, North Central Research
    Station. 55 p.

Gough, R.J. 1997. **Farming the cutover: a social history of Northern
    Wisconsin, 1900–1940.** Lawrence, KS: University Press of Kansas. 295 p.

Graham, R.T.; McCaffrey, S.; Jain, T.B. 2004. **Science basis for changing
    forest structure to modify wildfire behavior and severity.** Gen. Tech.
    Rep. RMRS-120. Fort Collins, CO: U.S. Department of Agriculture, Forest
    Service, Rocky Mountain Research Station. 43 p.

Greenberg, C.H.; Miller, S.; Waldrop, T.A. 2007. **Short-term response of shrews to prescribed fire and mechanical fuel reduction in a Southern Appalachian upland hardwood forest.** Forest Ecology and Management. 243: 231-236

Greenberg, C.H.; Otis, D.L.; Waldrop, T.A. 2006. **Response of white-footed mice *(Peromyscus leucopus)* to fire and fire surrogate fuel reduction treatments in a southern Appalachian hardwood forest.** Forest Ecology and Management. 234:355-362.

Greenberg, C.H.; Waldrop, T.A. 2008. **Short-term response of reptiles and amphibians to prescribed fire and mechanical fuel reduction in a southern Appalachian upland hardwood forest.** Journal of Wildlife Management. 255: 2883-2893.

Guries, R.P. 2002. *Pinus resinosa.* In: Pines of silvicultural importance. New York, NY: CABI Publishing: 379-391.

Guynn, D.C., Jr.; Guynn, S.T.; Wigley, T.B.; Miller, D.A. 2004. **Herbicides and forest biodiversity – what do we know and where do we go from here?** Wildlife Society Bulletin. 32:1085-1092.

Haight R.G.; Cleland D.T.; Hammer R.B.; Radeloff V.C.; Rupp T.S. 2004. **Assessing fire risk in the wildland–urban interface.** Journal of Forestry. 102(7), 41-48.

Haney, A.; Apfelbaum, S.; Burrins, J.M. 2008. **Thirty years of post-fire succession in a southern boreal forest bird community.** American Midland Naturalist. 159: 421-433.

Hansen, M.; Brand, G. 2006. **Michigan's forest resources in 2004.** Resource Bulletin NC-255. St Paul, MN: U.S. Department of Agriculture, Forest Service, North Central Research Station. 43 p.

Hauser, A.S. 2008. *Pinus resinosa.* In: Fire effects information system. Ft. Collins, CO: U.S. Department of Agriculture, Forest Service, Rocky Mountain Research Station Available at http://www.fs.fed.us/database/feis/plants/tree/pinres/all.html. (Accessed: September 9, 2011).

Heinselman, M.L. 1973. **Fire in the virgin forests of the Boundary Waters Canoe Area,** Minnesota. Quaternary Research. 3:329-382.

Hobson, K.A.; Schieck, J. 1999. **Changes in bird communities in boreal mixedwood forest: harvest and wildfire effects over 30 years.** Ecological Applications. 9: 849-863.

Hood, G.A.; Bayley, S.E.; Olson, W. 2007. **Effects of prescribed fire on habitat of beaver** *(Castor canadensis)* **in Elk Island National Park, Canada.** Forest Ecology and Management. 239: 200-209.

Hungerford, R.D.; Harrington, M.G.; Frandsen, W.H.; Ryan, K.C.; Niehoff, G.J. 1991. **Influence of fire on factors that affect site productivity.** In: Harvey, A. E.; Neuenschwander, F. L., comps. Proceedings-Management and productivity of western-montane forest soils. Ogden, Utah: U.S. Department of Agriculture, Forest Service, Intermountain Research Station: 32-50 p.

Hunter, M.E.; Shepperd, W.D.; Lentile, J.E.; Lundquist, J.E.; Andreu, M.G.; Butler, J.L.; Smith, F.W. 2007. **A comprehensive guide to fuels treatment practices for ponderosa pine in the Black Hills, Colorado Front Range, and Southwest.** Gen. Tech. Rep. RMRS-198. Fort Collins, CO: U.S. Department of Agriculture, Forest Service, Rocky Mountain Research Station. 93 p.

Hutto, R.L. 1995. **Composition of bird communities following stand-replacement fires in northern Rocky Mountain (U.S.A.) conifer forests.** Conservation Biology. 9: 1041-1058.

Irwin, L.L. 1975. **Deer-moose relationships on a burn in northeastern Minnesota.** Journal of Wildlife Management. 39: 653-662.

Johnson, J.B.; Edwards, J.W.; Ford, W.M.; Gates, J.E. 2009. **Roost tree selection by northern myotis (***Myotis septentrionalis***) maternity colonies following prescribed fire in a central Appalachian mountains hardwood forest.** Forest Ecology and Management. 258: 233-242.

Jones, B.; Fox, S.F.; Leslie, D.M.; Jr., Engle, D.M.; Lochmiller, R.L. 2000. **Herpetofaunal responses to brush management with herbicide and fire.** Journal of Range Management. 53: 154-158.

Jones, D.D.; Conner, L.M.; Storey, T.H.; Warren, R.J. 2004. **Prescribed fire and raccoon use of longleaf pine forests: implications for managing nest predation.** Wildlife Society Bulletin. 32: 1255-1259.

Jones, P.D.; Mixon, M.R.; Demarais, S. 2009. **Habitat quality following mid-rotation treatment in conservation reserve program pines.** Journal of Wildlife Management. 73: 1166-1173.

Kalcounis, M.C.; Hobson, K.A.; Brigham, R.M.; Hecker, K.R. 2008. **Bat activity in the boreal forest: Importance of stand type and vertical strata.** Journal of Mammalogy. 80: 673-682.

Karamanski, T. 1989. **Deep woods frontier: a history of logging in northern Michigan.** Detroit, MI: Wayne State University Press. 305 p.

Keane, R.E.; Agee, J.K.; Fule, P.; Keeley, J.E.; Key, C.; Kitchen, S.G.; Miller, R.; Schulte, L.A. 2008. **Ecological effects of large fires on US landscapes: benefit or catastrophe?** International Journal of Wildland Fire. 17:696-712.

Kent, B.; Gebert, K.; McCaffrey, S.; Martin, W.; Calkin, D.; Schuster, E.; Martin, I.; Bender, H.W.; Alward, G.; Kumagai, Y.; Cohn, P.; Carroll, M.S.; Williams, D.; Ekarius, C. 2003. **Social and economic issues of the Hayman Fire.** In: Graham, R.T., ed. Hayman fire case study. Gen. Tech. Rep. RMRS-114. Odgen, UT: U.S. Department of Agriculture, Forest Service, Rocky Mountain Research Station: 315-395.

Keith, L.B.; Surrendi, D.C. 1971. **Effects of fire on a snowshoe hare population.** Journal of Wildlife Management. 35: 16-26.

King, S.L.; Stribling, H.L.; Speake, D. 1991. **Cottontail rabbit initial responses to prescribed burning and cover enhancement.** Journal of the Alabama Academy of Science. 62: 178-188.

Kirkland, G.L., Jr.; Snoody, H.W.; Amsler, T.L. 1996. **Impact of fire on small mammals and amphibians in a central Appalachian deciduous forest.** American Midland Naturalist. 135: 253-260.

Kneeshaw, K.; Vaske, J.J.; Bright, A.D.; Absher, J.D., 2004. **Situational influences of acceptable wildland fire management actions.** Society & Natural Resources. 17(6): 477-489.

Koivula, M.J.; Schmiegelow, F.K.A. 2007. **Boreal woodpecker assemblages in recently burned forested landscapes in Alberta, Canada: effects of post-fire harvesting and burn severity.** Forest Ecology and Management. 242: 606-618.

Koprowski, J.L.; Leonard, K.M.; Zugmeyer, C.A.; Jolley; J.L. 2006. **Direct effects of fire on endangered Mount Graham red squirrels.** The Southwestern Naturalist. 51: 59-63.

Kotliar, N.B.; Kennedy, P.L.; Ferree; K. 2007. **Avifaunal responses to fire in southwestern montane forests along a burn severity gradient.** Ecological Applications. 17: 491-507.

Kreisel, K.J.; Stein, S.J. 1999. **Bird use of burned and unburned coniferous forests during winter.** The Wilson Bulletin. 111: 243-250.

Lacki, M.J.; Cox, D.R.; Dodd, L.E.; Dickinson, M.D. 2009. **Response of northern bats (Myotis septentrionalis) to prescribed fires in eastern Kentucky forests.** Journal of Mammalogy. 90: 1165-1175.

Lang, J.D.; Powell, A.; Krementz, D.G.; Conroy, M.J. 2002. **Wood thrush movements and habitat use: effects of forest management for red-cockaded woodpeckers.** The Auk. 119: 109-124.

Lim, S.H.; Bowker, J.M.; Johnson, C.Y.; Cordell, H.K. 2009. **Perspectives on prescribed fire in the South: Does ethnicity matter?** Southern Journal of Applied Forestry. 33(1): 17-24.

Loeb, S.C.; Waldrop, T.A. 2007. **Bat activity in relation to fire and fire surrogate treatments in southern pine stands.** Forest Ecology and Management. 255: 3185-3192.

Long, R.A.; Rachlow, J.L.; Kie, J.G. 2008. **Effects of season and scale on response of elk and mule deer to habitat manipulation.** Journal of Wildlife Management. 72: 1133-1142.

Long, R.A.; Rachlow, J.L.; Kie, J.G. 2009. **Sex-specific responses of North American elk to habitat manipulation.** Journal of Mammalogy. 90: 423-432.

Loomis, J.B.; Bair, L.S.; Gonzalez-Caban, A. 2001. **Prescribed fire and public support: Knowledge gained, attitudes changed in Florida.** Journal of Forestry. 99(11): 18-22.

Loope, W.L.; Anderton, J.B., 1998. **Human vs. lightning ignition of presettlement surface fires in coastal pine forests of the upper Great Lakes.** American Midland Naturalist. 140: 206-218.

Lorimer C.G.; Gough, W.R. 1988. **Frequency of drought and severe fire weather in north-eastern Wisconsin.** Journal of Environmental Management. 26: 203-219.

Magoun, A.J. 1997. **Selection of post-fire seres by lynx and showshoe hares in the Alaskan taiga.** Northwestern Naturalist. 78: 77-86.

Main, M.B.; Richardson, L.W. 2002. **Response of wildlife to prescribed fire in southwest Florida pine flatwoods.** Wildlife Society Bulletin. 30:213-221.

Marshall, J.D.; Blair J.M.; Peters, D.P.C.; Okin, G.; Rango, A.; Williams, M. 2008. **Predicting and understanding ecosystem responses to climate change at continental scales.** Frontiers in Ecology and the Environment. 6:273-280.

Martell, A.M. 1984. **Changes in small mammal communities after fire in northcentral Ontario.** The Canadian Field-Naturalist. 98:223-226.

Martin, S.L.; Theimer, T. C.; Fulé, P.Z. 2005. **Ponderosa pine restoration and turkey roost site use in northern Arizona.** Wildlife Society Bulletin. 33:859-864.

Matthews, C.E.; Moorman, C.E.; Greenberg, C.H.; Waldrop, T.A. 2008. **Response of reptiles and amphibians to repeated fuel reduction treatments.** Journal of Wildlife Management. 74:1301-1310.

Matthews, C.E.; Moorman, C.E.; Greenberg, C.H.; Waldrop, T.A. 2009. **Response of soricid populations to repeated fire and fuel reduction in the southern Appalachian mountains.** Forest Ecology and Management. 257:1939-1944.

McCaffrey, S. 2006. **Prescribed fire: What influences public approval?** In: Dickinson, M.B., ed. Fire in eastern oak forests: delivering science to land managers.Gen. Tech. Rep. NRS-P-1. Newtown Square, PA: U.S. Department of Agriculture, Forest Service, Northern Research Station: 192-198.

McCaffrey, S. 2008. **The homeowner view of thinning methods for fire hazard reduction: More positive than many think.** In: Narog, M.G., ed. Proceedings U.S. Department of Agriculture 2002 Fire Conference: Managing fire and fuels in the remaining wildlands and open spaces of the Southwestern United States. Gen. Tech. Rep. PSW-189. Albany, CA: U.S. Department of Agriculture, Forest Service, Pacific Southwest Research Station: 15-22.

McCaffrey, S.; Moghaddas, J.J.; Stephens, S.L. 2008. **Different interest group views of fuels treatments: Survey results from fire and fire surrogate treatments in a Sierran mixed conifer forest,** California, USA. International Journal of Wildland Fire. 17(2):224-233.

McCaffrey, S.M.;Olsen, C.S. 2012. **Research perspectives on the public and fire management: a synthesis of current social science on eight essential questions.** Gen. Tech. Rep. NRS-104. Newtown Square, PA: U.S. Department of Agriculture, Forest Service, Northern Research Station. 40 p.

McEwan, R.W.; Hutchinson, T.F.; Ford, R.D.; McCarthy B.C. 2007. **An experimental evaluation of fire history reconstruction using dendrochronology in white oak (*Quercus alba*).** Canadian Journal of Forest Research. 37:806-816.

McLeod, R.F.; Gates, E.J. 1998. **Response of herpetofaunal communities to forest cutting and burning at Chesapeake Farms, Maryland.** American Midland Naturalist. 139:164-177.

McNab, W.H.; Cleland, D.T.; Freeouf, J.A.; Keys, J.E.; Nowacki, G.J.;
Carpenter, C.A. 2007. **Description of ecological subregions: sections of the
conterminous United States.** Gen. Tech. Rep. WO-76B. Washington, DC:
U.S. Department of Agriculture, Forest Service. 80 p.

McRae, D.J. 1979. **Prescribed burning in jack pine logging slash: A review.**
Report 0-X-289. Sault Ste. Marie, ON: Canadian Forestry Service,
Department of the Environment, Great Lakes Research Centre.

McRae, D.J.; Lynham T.J.; French. R.J. 1994. **Understory prescribed burning
in red pine and white pine.** Forestry Chronicle. 70:395-401.

Meek, M.G.; Cooper, S.M.; Owens, K.M.; Cooper, R.M.; Wappel, A.L.
2008. **White -tailed deer distribution in response to patch burning on
rangeland.** Journal of Arid Environments. 72:2026-2033.

Methven, I.R. 1971. **Prescribed fire, crown scorch and mortality: field and
laboratory studies on red and white pine.** Ottawa, Canada: Canadian
Forestry Service, Department of the Environment.

Meyer, M.D.; Kelt, D.A.; North, M.P. 2007. **Microhabitat associations of the
northern flying squirrels in burned and thinned forest stands of the
Sierra Nevada.** American Midland Naturalist. 157:202-211.

Michael, E.; Thornburgh, P.I. 1971. **Immediate effects of hardwood removal
and prescribed burning on bird populations.** The Southwest Naturalist.
15:359-370.

Miles, P.D.; Brand G.J.; Mielke, M.E. 2004. **Minnesota's forest resources in
2003.** Resour. Bull. NC-246. U.S. St. Paul, MN: Department of Agriculture,
Forest Service, North Central Research Station.

Miller, W.E. 1978. **Use of prescribed burning in seed production areas to
control red pine cone beetle.** Environmental Entomologist. 7:698-702.

Mixon, M.R.; Demarais, S.; Jones, P.D.; Rude, B.J. 2009. **Deer forage response
to herbicide and fire in mid-rotation pine plantations.** Journal of Wildlife
Management. 73:663-688.

Monroe, M.C.; Pennisi, L.; McCaffrey, S.; Mileti, D. 2006. **Social science
to improve fuels management: A synthesis of research relevant to
communicating with homeowners about fuels management.** Gen. Tech.
Rep. NC-257. St. Paul, MN: U.S. Department of Agriculture, Forest Service,
North Central Research Station.

Moseley, K.R.; Castleberry, S.B.; Schweitzer, S.H. 2010. **Effects of prescribed
fire on herpetofauna in bottomland hardwood forest.** Southeastern
Naturalist. 2:475-486.

Murphy, E.C.; Lehnhausen, W.A. 1998. **Density and foraging ecology of woodpeckers following a stand-replacement fire.** The Journal of Wildlife Management. 62:1359-1372.

Myer, G. 2012. **Characterizing the decision process of land managers when managing for endangered species of fire dependent ecosystems: the case of the kirtland's warbler (*Septophaga kirtlandii* Baird).** Columbus, OH: Ohio State University. 84 p. M.S. thesis.

Nappi, A.; Drapeau, P. 2009. **Reproductive success of the black-backed woodpecker (*Picoides arcticus*) in burned boreal forests: Are burns source habitats?** Biological Conservation. 142:1381-1391.

National Interagency Fire Center (NIFC). 2010. **Wildland fire statistics.** Boise, ID: National InteragencyFire Center. Available at www.nifc.gov/fire_info/fire_stats.htm. (Accessed: Jan. 20, 2011).

Neumann, D.D.; Dickmann, D.I. 2001. **Surface burning in a mature stand of Pinus resinosa and Pinus strobus in Michigan: Effects on understory vegetation.** International Journal of Wildland Fire. 10:91-101.

Nowacki, G.J.; Abrams, M.D. 2008. **The demise of fire and "mesophication" of forests in the eastern United States.** Bioscience. 58:123-138.

Palik, B.J.; Zasada, J.C. 2003. **An ecological context for regenerating multi-cohort, mixed-species red pine forests.** Res. Note NC-382. St. Paul, MN: U.S. Department of Agriculture, Forest Service, North Central Forest Experiment Station. 8 p.

Paragi, T.F.; Johnson, D.D.; Katnik, D.D.; Magoun, A.J. 1996. **Marten selection of postfire seres in the Alaskan taiga.** Canadian Journal of Zoology. 74:2222-2237.

Passavoy, David M.; Fulé, Peter Z. 2006. **Snag and woody debris dynamics following severe wildfires in northern Arizona ponderosa pine forests.** Forest Ecology and Management. 223:237-246.

Peek, J.M. 1974. **Initial response of moose to a forest fire in northeastern Minnesota.** American Midland Naturalist. 91:435-438.

Perry, C.H. 2006. **Wisconsin's forest resources in 2004.** Resour. Bull. NC-261. St. Paul, MN: U.S. Department of Agriculture, Forest Service, North Central Research Station. 34 p.

Perry, R.W.; Rudolph, C.D.; Thill, R.E. 2009. **Reptile and amphibian responses to restoration of fire-maintained woodlands.** Restoration Ecology. 17:917-927.

Pilliod, D.S.; Bull, E.L.; Hayes, J.L.; Wales, B.C. 2006. **Wildlife and invertebrate response to fuel reduction treatments in dry coniferous forests of the western United States: a synthesis.** Gen. Tech. Rep. RMRS-173. Fort Collins, CO: U.S. Department of Agriculture, Forest Service, Rocky Mountain Research Station. 34 p.

Radeloff, V.C.; Hammer, R.B.; Stewart, S.I. 2005. **Rual and suburban sprawl in the U.S. Midwest from 1940 to 2000 and its relation to forest fragmentation.** Conservation Biology. 19:793-805.

Rempel, R.S.; Rogers, A.R.; Gluck, M.J. 1997. **Timber-management and natural-disturbance effects on moose habitat: Landscape evaluation.** Journal of Wildlife Management. 61:517-524.

Rouse, C. 1988. **Fire effects in northeastern forests: red pine.** Gen. Tech. Report NC-129. St. Paul, MN: U.S. Department of Agriculture, Forest Service, North Central Forest Experiment Station. 9 p.

Rudolf, P.O. 1990. *Pinus resinosa* **Ait.** In: Burns, R.M.; Honkala, B.H.,tech. coords. Silvics of North America. Volume 1. Conifers. Agric. Hndbk. 654. Washington, DC: U.S. Department of Agriculture, Forest Service: 442-455.

Russell, R.E.; Lehmkuhl, J.F.; Buckland, S.T.; Saab, V.A. 2008. **Short-term responses of red squirrels to prescribed burning in the interior pacific northwest, USA.** Journal of Wildlife Management. 74:12-17.

Ryan, K.C.; N.V. Noste. 1983. **Evaluating prescribed fires.** In: Lotan, J.E; Kilgore, B.M.; Fischer, W.C.; Mutch, R.W., tech. coords. In: Symposium and workshop of wilderness fire. Gen. Tech. Rep. INT-182. Ogden, UT. U.S. Department of Agriculture, Forest Service, Intermountain Research Station: 230-238.

Ryan, K.C.; E.D. Reinhardt. 1988. **Predicting postfire mortality of seven western conifers.** Canadian Journal of Forest Research 18:1291-1297.

Ryan, R.L.; Wamsley, M.B. 2006. **Perceptions of wildfire threat and mitigation measures by residents of fire-prone communities in the Northeast: survey results and wildland fire management implications.** In: McCaffrey, S.M., ed. The public and wildland fire management: social science findings for managers. Gen. Tech. Rep. NRS-1. Newton Square, PA: U.S. Department of Agriculture, Forest Service, Northern Research Station: 11-17.

Ryan, R.L.; Wamsley, M.B.; Blanchard, B.P. 2006. **Perceptions of wildfire threat and mitigation measures by residents of fire-prone communities in the Northeast: survey results and wildland fire management implications.** In: McCaffrey, S.M., ed. The public and wildland fire management: social science findings for managers. Gen. Tech. Rep. GTR-NRS-1. Newtown Square, PA: U.S. Department of Agriculture, Forest Service, Northern Research Station: 11-17.

Saab, V.A.; Powell, H.D.W. 2005. **Fire and avian ecology in North America: Process influencing pattern.** In: Saab, V.; Powell, H., eds. Fire and avian ecology in North America. Studies in Avian Biology. 30: 1-13.

Sansberg, D.V.; Ottmar, R.D.; Cushon, G.H. 2001. **Characterizing fuels in the 21st century.** International Journal of Wildland Fire. 10:381-387.

Scharbon, J.M.; Fauth, J.E. 2003. **Effects of prescribed burning on amphibian diversity in a southeastern U.S. National forest.** Conservation Biology. 17:1338-1349.

Scheller, R.M.; Tuyl, V.; Clark, K.; Hayden, N.G.; Hom, J; Mladenoff, D.J. 2008. **Simulation of forest change in the New Jersey Pine Barrens under current and pre-colonial conditions.** Forest Ecology and Management. 255:1489-1500.

Schulte, L.A.; Mladenoff, D.J.; Crow, T.R.; Merrick, L.C.; Cleland, D.T. 2007. **Homogenization of northern U.S. Great Lakes forest due to land use.** Landscape Ecology. 22:1089-1103.

Schulte, L.A.; Niemi, G.J. 1998. **Bird communities of early-successional burned and logged forest.** The Journal of Wildlife Management. 62:1418-1429.

Schwartz, C.C.; Franzmann, A.W. 1991. **Interrelationship of black bears to moose and forest succession in the northern coniferous forest.** Wildlife Monographs. 113:3-58.

Shindler, B.; Brunson, M.; Stankey, G.H. 2002. **Social acceptability of forest conditions and management practices: a problem analysis.** Gen. Tech. Rep. PNW-537. Portland, OR: U.S. Department of Agriculture, Forest Service, Pacific Northwest Research Station. 68 p.

Shindler, B.; Toman, E. 2003. **Fire reduction strategies in forest communities: A longitudinal analysis.** Journal of Forestry. 101(6):8-15.

Shindler, B.A.; Toman, E.; McCaffrey , S.M. 2009. **Public perspective of fire, fuels, and the Forest Service in the Great Lakes region: A survey of citizen-agency communication and trust.** International Journal of Wildland Fire. 18:157-164.

Simon, N.P.P.; Stratton, C.B.; Forbes, G.J.; Schwab, F.E. 2002. **Similarity of small mammal abundance in post-fire and clearcut forests.** Forest Ecology and Management. 165:163-172.

Smucker, K.M.; Hutto, R.L.; Steele, B.M. 2005. **Changes in bird abundance after wildfire: importance of fire severity and time since fire.** Ecological Applications. 15:1535-1549.

Sousa, W.P. 1984. **The role of disturbance in natural communities.** Annual Review of Ecology and Systematics. 15:353-391.

Stankey, G.H. 1976. **Wilderness fire policy: An investigation of visitor knowledge and beliefs.** Res. Pap. INT-180. Ogden, UT: U.S. Department Agriculture, Forest Service, Intermountain Forest and Range Experiment Station. 32 p.

Starker, T.J. 1934. **Fire resistance in the forest.** Journal of Forestry. 32:462-467.

Stearns, F.W. 1997. **History of the Lake States forests: natural and human impacts.** In: Vasievich, J.; Webster, M.; Henry, H., eds. Lake States regional forest resources assessment: technical papers. Gen. Tech. Rep. NC-189. St. Paul, MN: U.S. Department of Agriculture, Forest Service, North Central Forest Experiment Station: 8-29.

Steelman, T.; McCaffrey, S. 2011. **What is limiting more flexible fire management - public or agency pressure?** Journal of Forestry. 109(8):454-461.

Stratman, M.R.; Pelton, M.R. 2007. **Spatial response of American black bears to prescribed fire in northwest Florida.** Ursus. 18:62-71.

Sturtevant, B.R.; Miranda, B.R.; Yang, J.; He, H.S.; Gustafson, E.J.; Scheller, R.M. 2009. **Studying fire mitigation strategies in multi-ownership landscapes: balancing the management of fire-dependent ecosystems and fire risk.** Ecosystems. 12:445-461.

Sucoff, E.I.; Allison, J.H. 1968. **Fire defoliation and survival in a 47-year old red pine plantation.** Minnesota Forestry Research Note 187. St. Paul, MN: University of Minnesota, School of Forestry. 2 p.

Sullivan, T.P.; Lautenschlager, R.A.; Wagner, R.G. 1999. **Clearcutting and burning of northern spruce-fir forests: implications for small mammal communities.** Journal of Applied Ecology. 36:327-344.

Sullivan, T.P.; Sullivan, D.S.; Lindgren, P.M.F.; Boateng, J.O. 2002. **Influence of conventional and chemical thinning on stand structure and diversity of plant and mammal communities in young lodgepole pine forest.** Forest Ecology and Management. 170:173-187.

Sunquist, M.E. 1967. **Effects of fire on raccoon behavior.** Journal of Mammalogy. 48:673-674.

Swain, A.M. 1980. **Landscape patterns and forest history in the Boundary Waters Canoe Area, Minnesota: a pollen study from Hug Lake.** Ecology. 61(4):747-754.

Tiedemann, A.; Klemmedson, J.; Bull, E. 2000. **Solution of forest health problems with prescribed fire: are forest productivity and wildlife at risk?** Forest Ecology and Management. 127:1-18.

Toman, E.; Shindler, B.; Absher, J.; McCaffrey, S. 2008. **Postfire communications: the influence of site visits on local support.** Journal of Forestry. 106(1):25-30.

Toman, E.; Shindler, B.; Brunson, M. 2006. **Fire and fuel management communication strategies: citizen evaluations of agency outreach activities.** Society & Natural Resources. 19(4):321-336.

Toman, E.; Stidham, M.; Shindler, B.; McCaffrey, S. 2011. **Reducing fuels in the wildland urban interface: community perceptions of agency fuels treatments.** International Journal of Wildland Fire. 20(3):340-349.

Toman, E.; Stidham, M.; Shindler, B.; McCaffrey, S. 2013. **Social science at the wildland-urban interface: a compendium of research results.** Gen. Tech. Rep. NRS-111. Newton Square, PA: U.S. Department of Agriculture, Forest Service, Northern Research Station. 75 p.

Ucitel, D.; Christian, D.P.; Graham, J.M. 2003. **Vole use of coarse woody debris and implications for habitat and fuel management.** Journal of Wildlife Management. 67:65-72.

U.S. Forest Service (USFS). 2003. **Influence of forest structure on wildfire behavior and the severity of its effects: an overview.** Gen. Tech. Rep. RMRS-42-Volume 2. Ogden, UT: U.S. Department of Agriculture Forest Service, Rocky Mountain Research Station. 52 p.

Van Dyke, F.; Darragh, J.A. 2007. **Response of elk to changes in plant production and nutrition following prescribed burning.** Journal of Wildlife Management. 71:23-29.

Van Wagner, C.E. 1963. **Prescribed burning experiments: red and white pine.** Publ. No. 1020. Ottawa, Canada: Department of Forestry, Forestry Research Branch. 27 p.

Van Wagner, C.E. 1970. **Fire and red pine.** In: Fire ecology in the northern U.S. and Canada: proceedings of the tenth annual tall timbers fire ecology conference; 1970 April 20-21; Fredericton, NB. Tallahassee, FL: Tall Timbers Research Station: 211-219.

Van Wagner, C.E. 1972. **Duff consumption by fire in eastern pine stands.** Canadian Journal of Forest Research. 2:34-39.

Van Wagner, C.E. 1978. **Age-class distribution and the forest fire cycle.** Canadian Journal of Forest Research. 8:220-227

Vierling, K.; Lentile, L. 2006. **Red-headed woodpecker nest-site selection and reproduction in mixed ponderosa pine and aspen woodland following fire.** The Condor. 108:957-962.

Vining, J.; Merrick, M.S. 2008. **The influence of proximity to a national forest on emotions and fire-management decisions.** Environmental Management. 41(2):155-167.

Vogl, R.J. 1970. **Fire and the northern Wisconsin pine barrens.** In: Fire ecology in the northern U.S. and Canada: proceedings of the tenth annual tall timbers fire ecology conference; 1970 April 20-21; Fredericton, NB. Tallahassee, FL: Tall Timbers Research Station: 175-209.

Vogt, C.; Winter, G.; Fried, J.S. 2005. **Predicting homeowners' approval of fuel management at the wildland-urban interface using the theory of reasoned action.** Society & Natural Resources. 18(4):337-354.

Vogt, C.; Winter, G.; McCaffrey, S. 2007. **Community views of fuels management: are national forest local recreation users more supportive?** In: Burns, R.; Robinson, K., eds. Proceedings of the 2006 northeast recreation research symposium: proceedings of the symposium; 2006 April 9-11; Bolton Landing, NY. Gen. Tech. Rep. NRS-P-14. Newton Square, PA: U.S. Department of Agriculture, Forest Service, Northern Research Station: 546-550.

Walmsley, J.D.; Jones, D.L.; Reynolds, B.; Price M.H.; Healey, J.R. 2009. **Whole tree harvesting can reduce second rotation forest productivity.** Forest Ecology and Management. 257(3):1104-1111.

Webster, B.J. 2008. **Response of the understory to low intensity prescribed burning or mechanical and herbicide treatment in a northern mesic eastern white pine (*Pinus strobus* L.) forest in the Menominee Nation, Wisconsin.** Stevens Point, WI: University of Wisconsin. M.S. thesis.

Whitney, G.G. 1986. **Relation of Michigan's presettlement forests to substrate and disturbance history.** Ecology. 67:1548-1559.

Whitney, G.G. 1987. **An ecological history of the Great Lakes forest of Michigan.** Journal of Ecology. 75:667-684.

Williams M. 1989. **Americans and their forests: a historical geography.** Cambridge, UK: Cambridge University Press. 599 p.

Wilson, R.S; Hix, D.M.; Goebel, P.C.; Corace, R.G., III 2009. **Identifying land manager objectives and alternatives for mixed-pine forest ecosystem management and restoration in eastern Upper Michigan.** Ecological Restoration. 27:4.

Winter, G.; Fried, J.S. 2000. **Homeowner perspectives on fire hazard, responsibility, and management strategies at the wildland-urban interface.** Society & Natural Resources. 13(1):33-49.

Winter, G.J.; Vogt, C.; Fried, J.S. 2002. **Fuel treatments at the wildland-urban interface: common concerns in diverse regions.** Journal of Forestry. 100(1):15-21.

Winter, G.; Vogt, C.; McCaffrey, S. 2006. **Residents warming up to fuels management: homeowners' acceptance of wildfire and fuels management in the wildland-urban interface.** In: McCaffrey, S.M., ed. The public and wildland fire management: social science findings for managers. Gen. Tech. Rep. NRS-1. Newtown Square, PA: U.S. Department of Agriculture, Forest Service, Northern Research Station: 19-32.

Woodall, C.W.; Charney, J.J.; Liknes, G.C.; Potter, B.E. 2005. **What is the fire danger now?** Linking fuel inventories with atmospheric data. Journal of Forestry. 103:293-298.

Yoder, J. 2008. **Liability, regulation, and endogenous risk: the incidence and severity of escaped prescribed fires in the United States.** Journal of Law & Economics. 51:294-325.

Zasada, J.C.; Palik, B.J.; Crow, T.R.; Gilmore, D.W. 2004. **Applications for silvicultural systems in the northern Great Lakes Region of the United Sates.** In: Perera, A.H.; Buse, L.J.; Weber, M.G., eds. Emulating natural forest landscape disturbances: concepts and applications. New York, NY: Columbia University Press: 230-242.

Zwolak, R.; Foresman, K.R. 2007. **Effects of a stand-replacing fire on small-mammal communities in montane forest.** Canadian Journal of Zoology. 85:815-822.

APPENDIX: SPECIES RESPONSE TO FIRE BY MAJOR TAXONOMIC GROUPS

We conducted a literature review for all faunal species mentioned in this report using the research databases JSTOR and EJC. We used simple restriction terms to reduce superfluous results. Specifically, advanced search options were used to remove journals not related to the biological sciences. Individual species were searched for using Boolean commands in the following format:

"common name" AND fire#
"common name" AND burn*

as well as

"scientific name" AND fire#
"scientific name" AND burn*

This resulted in four unique searches per species. Because the vast majority of bird species searched returned no relevant results, further searches were conducted using:

"boreal forest" AND fire# AND birds AND community
"boreal forest" AND burn* AND birds AND community
"laurentian mixed pine" AND fire# AND birds AND community
"laurentian mixed pine" AND burn* AND birds AND community
"boreal forest" AND fire# AND avian AND community
"boreal forest" AND burn* AND avian AND community
"laurentian mixed pine" AND fire# AND avian AND community
"laurentian mixed pine" AND burn* AND avian AND community

Results included here were limited based on relevance to the topic as well as the region and/or habitat type.

General Findings

We limited our review of wildlife response to fire to a traditional grouping of terrestrial vertebrates, including mammals, birds, reptiles and amphibians. Despite the limited published information specific to the Laurentian mixed-pine ecosystem, our meta-analysis revealed an overall trend across geographic regions and across taxa for positive responses to prescribed fire and fire use for some species. Notably, large game mammals such as the white-tailed deer (*Odocoileus virginanus*) and elk (*Cervus elaphus*) benefit from grassy understory conditions created by fire. Avian species also benefit from fire based fuels reduction, as species diversity tends to increase following fire use, with specific increases in cavity nesting species and woodpeckers. However, so little is known on the effects of prescribed fire and fire use on amphibians and reptiles within the Laurentian mixed-pine ecosystem that only limited conclusions can be drawn on their responses. Table 1 presents wildlife response to fire based on published literature by major taxonomic group. When articles describe response of multiple species or contain multiple species tables, such as response between seasons, each table was considered separately and thus may be represented more than once in Table 1.

Mammals

Chiroptera: Little research has been conducted on the effects of fire on bats; none has been done on bats in the Laurentian mixed-pine forests. Loeb and Waldrop (2007) provide the only current study analyzing the effects of recent fire on bat activity within pine stands. Their research indicates that bat activity is lower in thinned and burned stands than in thinned-only stands, and that there is only a marginal increase in activity in burned stands over control stands. Some evidence suggests that structural changes caused by wildfire may be beneficial for bats when there is a reduction in canopy structure and changes tree species composition (Kalcounis et al. 2008). Studies on the northern bat (*Myotis septentrionalis*) by Lacki et al. (2009) and Johnson et al. (2009) in deciduous forests have found no significant change in roosting habits or sizes of home ranges or core areas. However, these studies did find some changes in preference for roost sites with higher percentages of fire-killed stems and trees with greater percentage bark coverage. Generally, bats are highly sensitive to canopy clutter and individual species vary in clutter tolerance. Managers interested in specific species should consult the primary literature for information on specific habitat requirements. Additionally, individual species have different roosting requirements, and managers responsible for maintaining tree roosting bat species should consider the effect that burn intensity will have on snag availability and

Table 1.— Wildlife response to fire (article counts by type of fire)

	Total article counts (all types of fire)			Fire use			Prescribed fire		
	Positive	Neutral	Negative	Positive	Neutral	Negative	Positive	Neutral	Negative
Mammals	27	19	15	12	11	8	15	13	7
Birds*	21	12	6	10	2	8	7	10	2
Herpetofauna	5	5	5	-	-	-	4	5	4
Total	53	36	26	22	13	16	26	28	13

*Responses for birds are a mix of individual responses and community responses, including diversity changes.

take precautions to preserve known roost trees with areas scheduled for burns, as well as other suitable snags. In the absence of more studies on the effects of fire on chiropterans, land managers interested in managing for bats should consult literature on the relationship between forest structure, roost site availability, and bats.

Canidae: Few studies have been published on the effects of fire on canids; none have been published on canids in the Great Lakes region. No information on the effects of fire on foxes in this region were found in the literature. Within chaparral in Arizona, fire was found to have a negative impact on coyote immediately after the fire, but there was no significant change in use (Cunningham et al. 2006). In the sub-arctic taiga in Alaska, fire was found to have negative effects on wolves immediately after fire, but wolves' use of burned areas after 3 years was similar to that from before fire (Ballard et al 2000). Decreased use of burned habitat by wolves is likely due to decreased prey abundance (Ballard et al. 2000).

Felidae: Few studies have been published on the effects of fire on felids; none have been published on felids in the Great Lakes region. No published studies on the effects of fire on bobcats were found in the primary literature. In southern pine forests in Florida, recently burned areas (<1 year since burn) experienced 16.7 percent higher use by pumas than older burns (2 to 4 years since fire) (Dees et al. 2001). In contrast, lynx have been found to use middle-aged burns almost exclusively over recent or historic burns (Magoun 1997). Preferential use of middle-aged burns by lynx is attributed to snowshoe hare abundance, and managers interested in using fire in areas with lynx populations are encouraged to read the information on lagomorphs (Fox 1978).

Ursidae: Only a handful of studies on the effects of fire on black bears have been published in the primary literature. Schwartz and Franzmann (1991) provide the only study in the boreal forest, finding that black bears using recent wildfire burns exhibited greater weight and survival rates than those using older burns. However, other studies in southern pine forests and chaparral have found decreased fecundity and use of recently burned areas (Stratman and Pelton 2007, Cunningham and Ballard 2004, Cunningham et al. 2003). Within burned areas, Stratman and Pelton (2007) found that bears concentrated use in areas that were burned 3 years previously, and Cunningham et al. (2003) found that black bears exhibited increased use of unburned islands within burned areas, although bear use of burned areas increased each year after fire. Within burned areas, Cunningham and Ballard (2004) found a shift in sex ratio in bears >1 year old from a preburn ratio of 1:1 to 4:1 males to females, along with decreased reproductive rates and fecundity among females. In contrast, Schwartz and

Franzmann (1991) found a higher ratio of females to males in both recent and middle-aged burns, as well as an increased number in yearlings in the recent burn due to higher fecundity rates and survival. The most important factors in determining whether fire will have a positive or negative impact on black bears appear to be changes in food and cover availability, specifically in the availability of hard mast vs. soft mast and ungulate prey (Stratman and Pelton 2007, Cunningham et al. 2003, Schwartz and Franzmann 1991). In general, managers interested in treating areas with black bear populations with fire should consider the effects that fire will have on local food resources; it seems unlikely that prescribed fires in the boreal forest will reduce suitable cover enough for black bears to avoid burned areas. Managers interested in the effects of fire on black bears are strongly encouraged to read the monograph by Schwartz and Franzmann (1991), which contains a large quantity of relevant information.

Procyonidae: Little published information is available on the effects of fire on raccoons, but it appears that raccoons avoid burned areas; in longleaf pine forests, Jones et al. (2004) found raccoons were 62 percent more likely to use unburned stands. However, in an oak savanna in Minnesota, Sunquist (1967) found no alteration in raccoon behavior 4 days after fire.

Mustelidae: Information on mustelid response to fire is limited; no published studies could be found for individual species other than the American marten. Marten, it appears, may be negatively affected by fire (Paragi et al 1996). In particular, juvenile males have been found at higher densities in 6 to 9 year old burns than in surrounding mature forest, suggesting that these areas may act as population "sinks" (Paragi et al. 1996). However, when wildfire creates a diversity of habitats, fire may be beneficial to martens over time thorough increased cover and food types.

Lagomorpha: Little has been published regarding the effects of fire on lagomorphs. The effects of fire appear to be time dependent for snowshoe hare (Keith and Surrendi 1971, Magoun 1997). Negative responses by snowshoe hare appear to be limited to the first year after fire, as Keith and Surrendi (1971) found that snowshoe hares reoccupied burned areas in the year following wildfire. Similarly, (Magoun 1997) found that snowshoe hares used middle-aged burned areas more extensively than other burn ages. Conversely, King et al. (1991) found increases in cottontail abundance in the first 2 years following prescribed fire. Changes in use of burned areas by lagomorphs appear to be strongly influenced by cover availability and browse availability and type (Keith and Surrendi 1971, King et al. 1991, Magoun 1997). In boreal regions, managers concerned with snowshoe hare populations should pay particular attention to the availability of willow and aspen browse (Magoun 1997).

Castoridae: Only one published study on the relationship between fire and beaver could be found in the primary literature. From this single article, it appears that fire negatively impacts beaver, as the number of active beaver lodges and colonies on Elk Island National Park decreased following fire (Hood et al. 2007). Decreases in the number of active lodges and colonies appear to be related to decreased food availability due to increase herbivory by cervids (Hood et al. 2007).

Cervidae: A more substantial body of information is available for cervids, including some on cervids within the Great Lakes region. Strong evidence from these research articles suggests that fire is beneficial for all cervids in the Great Lakes region. In the boreal forest, white-tailed deer have been found to change their temporal use patterns of burned stands, increasing their use of burned aspen stands (Irwin 1975). Heavier use of burned aspen stands corresponds to the greatest output of biomass of available forest types post-fire, although use of coniferous stands increased in early spring and late fall (Irwin 1975). Similarly, in southern pine forests in Mississippi, recently burned areas were found to have improved foraging habitat with forb biomass approximately three times higher than unburned control plots (Jones et al. 2009, Mixon et al. 2009). However, in a rangeland habitat use of burned areas decreased after a spike in use 1 to 2 months post-fire (Meek et al. 2008). Use or avoidance of burned areas by white-tailed deer is strongly related to browse availability (Irwin 1975, Meek et al. 2008, Jones et al. 2009, Mixon et al. 2009).

Elk also respond favorably to fire, and have been found to increase foraging activity in burned areas in the 1 to 2 years following a burn (Van Dyke and Darragh 2007). Despite increased use of burned areas, Long et al. (2008) found that this preferential selection was strongest in spring, although elk exhibited no selection within home ranges. However, Long et al. (2009) found that males avoid all burned stands in spring, while burned stands were avoided or used in proportion to availability by both sexes. Increased use of burned areas is attributed to increased quantity and possibly increased quality of forage (Van Dyke and Darragh 2007, Long et al. 2009).

As with white-tailed deer and elk, moose also exhibit positive responses to burned areas. Peek (1974) found rapid migration of moose into burned areas while Rempel et al. (1997) found higher moose density in burned areas, particularly at edges. Irwin (1975) observed a change in temporal use of burned stands, with burned aspen stands receiving the most use, corresponding with increased biomass.

Scuiridae: Information on scuirids and their response to fire is extremely limited. Fire appears to negatively impact flying squirrels, likely due to decreases in food resources, although detection ability may be a factor (Meyer et al. 2007, Zwolak and Foresman 2007). Red squirrels have not been found to exhibit any strong response to fire, although the endangered subspecies Tamiasciurus hudsonicus grahamensis was observed to have a high (35 percent) direct mortality rate in a group of radio-collared individuals (Koprowski et al. 2006, Russell et al. 2008). Least chipmunks have been observed to increase in population size in fall following a burn (Martell 1984), although as a group chipmunks have not been found to exhibit any strong response to fire (Zwolak and Foresman 2007).

Micromammals (*Soricidae, Muridae*): Micromammals vary widely in their response to fire, however, due to the large number of species within this group, family information has been briefly summarized according to general large trends.

Soricidae: Shrews do not appear to exhibit any negative response to fire, although based on cover preferences abundances of different species may be expected to change with time (Greenberg et al. 2007).

Muridae: Southern red-backed voles respond negatively to reductions in slash and cover caused by fire (Martel 1984, Simon et al. 2002, Sullivan et al. 1999, Zwolak and Foresman 2007). Meadow voles, in contrast, respond either positively to fire (Sullivan et al. 1999), or to exhibit no strong response (Geluso and Bragg 1986, Simon et al. 2002). Deer mice response to fire is well documented across a wide variety of different habitats, and in most habitat types (as represented by the National Fire and Fire Surrogate project) have been found to generally respond positively to fire (Converse et al. 2006). Indeed, deer mice have been found to be the most abundant small mammal in recently burned areas, accounting for as much as 64.7 percent of all rodents captured (Zwolak and Foresman 2007). So positive is the response of deer mice to fire that one study found population levels to expand 2 to 25 times that of preburn levels (Martell 1984).

Birds: The selection of birds included in this review is based largely on the list of birds provided by the Minnesota Department of Natural Resources at http://www. dnr.state.mn.us/animap/index.html. From this initial list, grassland birds were removed as well as birds that did not include in their home range the Laurentian mixed-pine ecosystem.

Avian communities: It is apparent that fire, whether prescribed or naturally ignited, can have some significant immediate effects on avian community structure (Apfelbaum and Haney 1981, Haney et al. 2008, Smucker et al. 2005). Although there have been few long-term studies on the effects of fire on birds, post-fire bird communities change significantly with time since burn (Bock et al. 1978, Hobson and Schieck 1999, Haney et al. 2008). Several of the studies reviewed found that post-fire avian communities exhibited an increase in species richness and abundance (Michael and Thornburgh 1971, Schulte and Niemi 1998, Smucker et al. 2005, Haney et al. 2008). Almost all found that the species composition shifted following fire; changes in community composition have been related in most cases to changes in habitat structure and food availability (Bock et al. 1978, Apfelbaum and Haney 1981, Blake 1982, Bock and Bock. 1983, Hutto 1995, Kreisel and Stein 1999, Smucker et al. 2005, Kotliar et al. 2007, Haney et al. 2008). Generally, fire reduces habitat closure, and an increase in open-foraging species occurs post-fire (Bock et al. 1978, Bock and Bock 1983). When fire severity is high and a large number of standing dead trees are created, bark foraging species also increase in number immediately post fire (Apfelbaum and Haney 1981, Hutto 1995, Hobson and Schieck 1999). Long-term studies indicate that species composition begins to resemble prefire communities as vegetation approaches prefire levels, however, species diversity may be higher than prefire levels (Hobson and Schieck 1999, Haney et al. 2008).

Woodpeckers: Woodpeckers, particularly those of the genus *Picoides*, respond rapidly to fire, colonizing burned areas in the year immediately following high intensity wildfires (Apfelbaum and Haney 1981, Hutto 1995, Koivula and Schmiegelow 2007, Haney et al. 2008). Densities of black-backed woodpeckers (*Picoides arcticus*) have been found to be higher than nearby unburned habitats, with densities exceeding 0.2 individuals /ha (Murphy and Lehnhausen 1998). Several studies have found that several species of woodpecker, including the black-backed woodpecker, hairy woodpecker (*Picoides villosus*), and red-headed woodpecker (*Melanerpes erythrocephalus*) select nest sites close to unburned habitats (Covert-Bratland et al. 2006, Vierling and Lentile 2006, Nappi and Drapeau 2009). Furthermore, nesting success of black-backed woodpeckers is higher in these areas (Nappi and Drapeau 2009). Densities of black-backed and three-toed woodpeckers in burned habitats peaks the year immediately post-fire, and decrease significantly 2 and 3 years post-fire (Murphy and Lehnhausen 1998, Nappi and Drapeau 2009). Hairy woodpeckers exhibit a similar pattern, with home ranges increasing with time since burn, and high-severity burn areas decreasing in importance between 3 and 6 years post-fire. In contrast to the improved nesting success of the *Picoides* woodpeckers, red-headed woodpecker has been found to have lower nest success in burned areas than that reported in unburned habitats (Vierling and Lentile 2006). This result should be interpreted cautiously however, as the study that found lower nesting success did not measure nesting success in unburned habitat, but compared the nesting success rate of their study to other studies. In general, woodpeckers respond favorably to wildfires that create an abundance of snags. However, it is unlikely that low intensity prescribed fires that do not create high densities of snags will illicit a response.

Grouse: Only two articles were found concerning grouse and fire; one for the spruce grouse (*Falcipennis canadensis*) and one for the sage grouse (*Centrocercus urophasianus*). High severity wildfire reduced spruce grouse densities from 97 birds/km^2 prefire to 40/km^2 post-fire (Elliston 1975). Furthermore, concentrations of spruce grouse were found in unburned habitat adjacent to burned habitat, and individuals banded in the burn area prior to fire were harvested by hunters up to 10 km from the study area (Elliston 1975). In contrast, sage grouse did not exhibit any response to prescribed fire (Fischer et al 1997).

Wood thrush: Only two articles were located that focused solely on the effects of fire on the wood thrush (*Hylocichla mustelina*). Low-intensity prescribed fires appear to have no significant positive or negative impact on this species (Lang et al. 2002, Artman and Downhower 2003). However, nesting locations in burned areas were in areas with greater canopy cover and higher moisture levels (Artman and Downhower 2003). Emigration from burned habitats may be expected to be lower than emigration from unburned habitats, with juveniles dispersing from burned habitat selecting densely covered hardwood habitats (Lang et al. 2002).

Wild turkey: Wild turkey (*Meleagris gallopavo*) appear to have a positive response to fire both in the short and long term. In the first few months after fire, turkey exhibit a preference for burned habitats (Main and Richardson 2002). Similarly, increased use of burned habitat by turkeys has been found in the years post-fire (Miller and Conner 2007). Merriam's wild turkey (*Meleagris gallopavo merriami*) exhibits no significant response to fire by roost site abundance or number of new roosts (Martin et al. 2005).

Herpetofauna: The effects of fire on herpetofauna in the Great Lakes region is largely unexplored; no specific studies were found that focus on this area. The bulk of the information on the effects of fire on herpetofauna comes from the southeastern and northwestern United States. The focus on these areas represents an unfortunate gap in the information available to forest managers in the Laurentian mixed-pine ecosystem trying to preserve herpetofaunal assemblages. To provide some relevant information on the effects of fire on herpetofauna, studies that include at least two species present in the Great Lakes region have been reviewed with the relevant species noted. In almost all cases these studies focus on species abundance, richness and evenness, rather than on individual species. The notable exception to this case is a study on the massasauga rattlesnake (*Sistrus catenatus*), by Durbian (2006), which found a deceased individual after a grassland fire; pre-fire mowing in preparation for the prescribed burn resulted in a mortality rate of 43 percent. However, due to the low sample size, the effects of fire in this case are unclear, beyond the author's suggestion to avoid mowing and burning while massasauga rattlesnake are active. Because no other articles focused on individual species, only select other species noted in other studies on herpetofaunal assemblages will be noted individually.

The bulk of the studies reviewed gave similar information on the effects of fire on herpetofauna, primarily, that fire had negative or no significant impacts on amphibians, and positive or no significant impacts on reptiles (McLeod and Edwards 1998, Jones et al. 2000, Greenberg and Waldrop 2008, Matthews et al. 2008, Perry et al. 2009, Moseley et al. 2010). More specifically, several studies have found that fire negatively affects several species of salamanders (Scharbon and Fauth 2003, Matthews et al. 2008). American toads (*Bufo americanus*) diverge notably from the negative or neutral trend in responses of amphibians, as Kirkland et al. (1996) and Greenberg and Waldrop (2008) both found increases in their abundance after fire; in the case of Kirkland et al. (1996) American toads accounted for 70.8 percent of all amphibian captures post-fire.

Explanations for the response of herpetofauna to fire, although covering a variety of measurable variables, are largely related to micro-site changes in cover and moisture. Amphibians likely exhibit negative responses to fire when micro-site characteristics after fire are more xeric than pre-fire conditions (Matthews et al. 2008). In contrast, reductions in canopy cover create basking opportunities for reptiles, which are more tolerant of xeric conditions (Matthews et al. 2008).

Toman, Eric; Hix, David M.; Goebel, P. Charles; Gehrt, Stanley D.; Wilson, Robyn S.;
    Sherry, Jennifer A.; Silvis, Alexander; Nyamai, Priscilla; Williams, Roger A.; McCaffrey,
    Sarah. 2014. **Hazardous fuels management in mixed red pine and eastern white
    pine forest in the northern Lake States: A synthesis of knowledge.** Gen. Tech.
    Rep. NRS-134. Newtown Square, PA: U.S. Department of Agriculture, Forest Service,
    Northern Research Station. 64 p.

Fuels reduction decisions are made within a larger context of resource management
characterized by multiple objectives including ecosystem restoration, wildlife management,
commodity production (from timber to nontraditional forest products), and provision of
recreation opportunities and amenity values. Implementation of fuels treatments is strongly
influenced by their perceived influence on and compatibility with overarching management
objectives. In some cases these objectives may be complementary while in others they
may involve difficult tradeoffs. Such tradeoffs are only further complicated by institutional
mandates, limited availability of information, and complex ownership patterns. Like natural
resource managers across the United States, those in the northern Lake States must
balance these competing demands as they seek to build their management programs.
However, there is limited information available to support these management decisions
in the mixed red (*Pinus resinosa* Ait.) and eastern white pine (*P. strobus* L.) forests of the
northern Lake States.

This report informs fuels management decisions in the northern Lake States by
synthesizing existing knowledge from the fields of silviculture, forest ecology, wildlife
ecology, forest economics, public acceptance, and decision science. We provide an
overview of forests and fire regimes in the northern Lake States followed by a description
of different fuels treatment techniques and their expected outcomes. We then include a
discussion of comprehensive management principles to consider in developing fire and
fuels management programs for the region.

KEY WORDS: Great Lakes mixed conifer, fuels reduction, prescribed fire, forest thinning

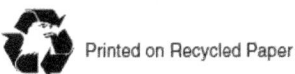 Printed on Recycled Paper

Northern Research Station

www.nrs.fs.fed.us